A CLASSICAL
STORYBOOK

A CLASSICAL STORYBOOK

SELECTED AND EDITED BY MORRIS BISHOP

DRAWINGS BY ALISON MASON KINGSBURY

CORNELL UNIVERSITY PRESS

ITHACA AND LONDON

880.8
B54m
72082
nov., 1970

First published 1970

International Standard Book Number 0-8014-0577-7
Library of Congress Catalog Card Number 76-121099
Printed in the United States of America by Kingsport Press, Inc.

PREFACE

MOST OF our literatures, even those of primitives like the North American Indians, began with song-stories, recited by bards to their own music. The song-story suffered fission; the song part became poetry; the story part descended to a lower, often subliterary level. A "mere story" is still sometimes discountenanced by poets, critics, and even fiction-writers. Everyone loves a story, but not everyone respects it.

The Greeks invented a whole world of story, a country above and below the earth, peopled by gods and demigods, each with his own defined character. In this land of gods and heroes their imaginations roved at will. Yet the Greeks could not overlook their own familiar background of mountains and rocky shores and storms at sea. They brought the gods to earth and with splendid realism told of legendary men and women.

Greek literature begins with Homer, who wrote the first and perhaps the greatest of song-stories, or epic poems. I have chosen the episode of Ulysses and Nausicaa as an example of Homer's romantic realism, and I have presented it in Samuel Butler's prose version. The song therein is muted, but the story, I think, is enhanced.

Nearly a millennium later there appeared the Milesian novelists, so called because their headquarters was the city of Miletus, in Asia Minor. Their tales mark the effective beginning in western culture of realistic imaginative prose. Their creators discovered the great formula of fiction: boy meets girl; boy and girl are parted; boy seeks girl through a myriad misadventures; boy recovers girl, and both live happily ever after.

Fortunately the Milesian Tales were read, preserved, and copied in the Greek-speaking Eastern Empire. Since the language did not change much, they were immediately accessible to readers. They are too little known in our times, and are unduly disesteemed by contrast with the poets, philosophers, dramatists, and historians of the classical age of Greece.

The Romans, like the Greeks, possessed an ample fund of story material, in the form of national legends and hero-tales. But the story seems to have enjoyed little prestige unless it was couched in the poetic form which has assured its persistence. I have ventured to render Virgil and Ovid in modern prose; the poetic loss may be somewhat compensated by prosaic gain.

Very little Latin prose fiction remains—indeed, only Petronius and Apuleius. The reasons are not far to seek. Popular, or Vulgar, Latin died, taking with it the ephemera of literature. Latin became a learned language, with a need to support its dignity. The fragile papyrus leaves of the first writers have disappeared. The monkish copyists preserved on parchment the works of the great poets and especially the theological disquisitions of the Church Fathers; they could hardly be expected to spend months setting down pagan bawdry and scurrilous tales on costly parchment. Thus only fragments of Petronius' *Satyricon* are extant; and thus Apuleius' *Golden Ass* survives in a single eleventh-century manuscript. Who could have been the scribe who stole time from his proper duties and parchment from the monastery stocks to rewrite the racy story?

The mere existence of Petronius and Apuleius, their competence in narrative and character-drawing, are evidence of a background of a Roman art of fiction, of a vast submerged literature. It is sad to think of all that has been lost; let us at least be grateful that something remains.

MORRIS BISHOP

Ithaca, New York
May 1970

CONTENTS

I THE GREEKS

Ulysses and Nausicaa, *by Homer*   3
Rhampsinitus and the Robbers, *by Herodotus*   21
The Ring of Polycrates, *by Herodotus*   25
Zopyrus, the Double Agent, *by Herodotus*   28
The Wooing of Agarista, *by Herodotus*   33
The Euboean Hunter, *by Dio Chrysostom*   36
Chaereas and Callirhoe, *by Chariton*   57
True History, *by Lucian*   83
Daphnis and Chloe, *by Longus*   99
An Ethiopian Story, *by Heliodorus*   116
Alexander, the Brahmins, and Queen Candace,
    by Pseudo-Callisthenes   141

II THE ROMANS

The Tragedy of Dido and Aeneas, *by Virgil*   159
Pyramus and Thisbe, *by Ovid*   189
Philemon and Baucis, *by Ovid*   193
Pygmalion, *by Ovid*   197
Trimalchio's Dinner, *by Petronius*   201
Thelyphron's Story, *by Apuleius*   217
The Story of the Gentlewoman, *by Apuleius*   226
Androclus and the Lion, *by Aulus Gellius*   243

I
THE GREEKS

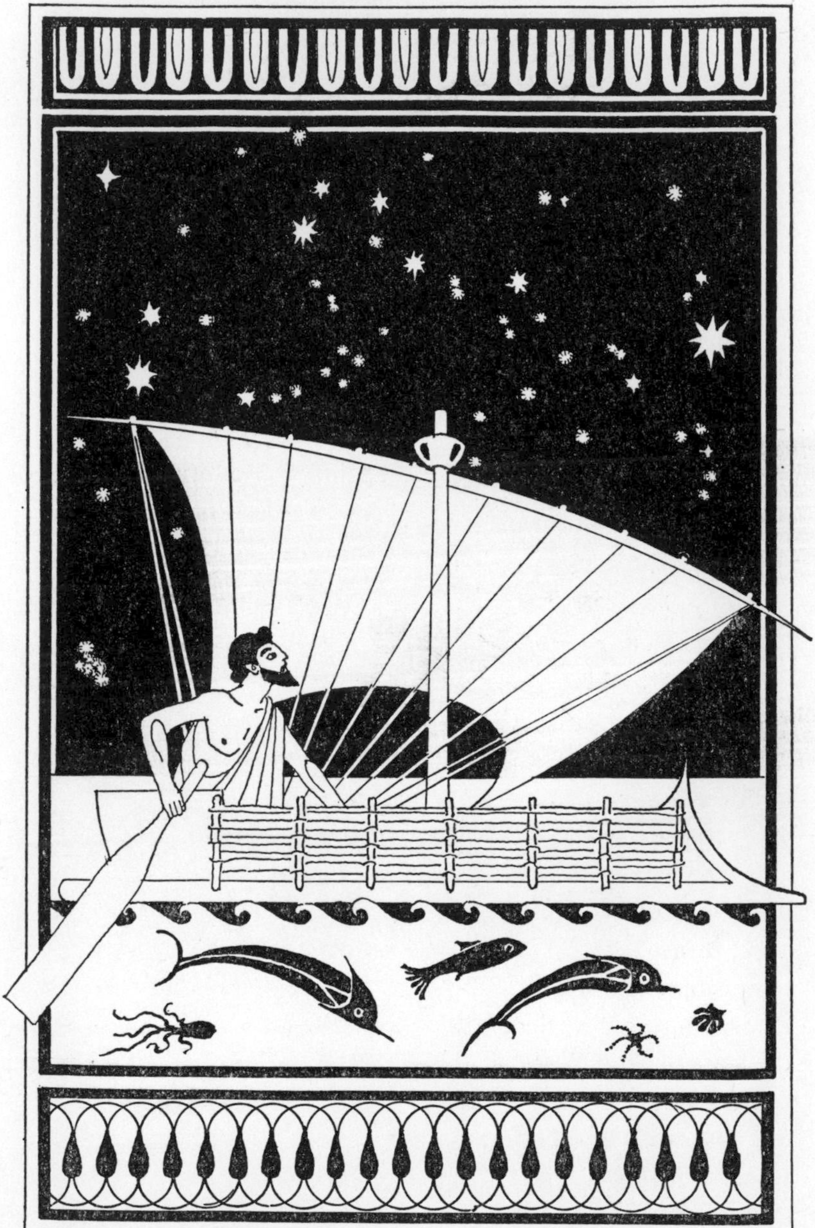

ULYSSES AND NAUSICAA

BY HOMER

Of Homer the poet we know nothing, not his time and place, not even his gender and number. Our ignorance of the author has not prevented scholars from writing many great books about him, her, or them. All that seems secure is that he, she, or they lived in the eighth century B.C. and composed the *Iliad* and the *Odyssey*, epic poems dealing with the Trojan War and its sequels in the Mycenaean age.

Our selection is an episode from the fifth and sixth books of the *Odyssey*. Ulysses, trying to find his way home to Ithaca, has been entertained for eight years by the goddess Calypso on her island of Ogygia. Parting from him by mutual consent, Calypso aids Ulysses to build a navigable raft.

The translation is by Samuel Butler, author of *The Way of All Flesh* and *Erewhon*. It was published by A. C. Fifield, in London, in 1900.

WHEN THE child of morning, rosy-fingered dawn, appeared, Ulysses put on his shirt and cloak, while the goddess wore a dress of a light gossamer fabric, very fine and graceful, with a beautiful golden girdle about her waist and a veil to cover her head. She at once set herself to think how she could speed Ulysses on his way. So she gave him a great bronze axe that suited his hands; it was sharpened on both sides, and had a beautiful olive-wood handle fitted firmly on to it. She also gave him a sharp adze, and then led the way to the far end of the island where the largest trees grew—alder, poplar, and pine, that reached the sky—very dry and well seasoned, so as to sail light for him in the water. Then, when she had shown him where the best trees grew, Calypso went home, leaving him to cut them, which he soon finished doing. He cut down twenty trees in all and adzed them smooth, squaring them by rule in good workmanlike fashion. Meanwhile Calypso came back with some augers, so he bored holes with them and fitted the timbers together with bolts and rivets. He made the raft as broad as a skilled shipwright makes the beam of a large vessel, and he fixed a deck on top of the ribs, and ran a gunwale all round it. He also made a mast with a yard arm, and a rudder to steer with. He fenced the raft all round with wicker hurdles as a protection against the waves, and then he threw on a quantity of wood. By and by Calypso brought him some linen to make the sails, and he made these too, excellently, making them fast with braces and sheets. Last of all, with the help of levers, he drew the raft down into the water.

In four days he had completed the whole work, and on the fifth Calypso sent him from the island after washing him and giving him some clean clothes. She gave him a goat skin full of black wine, and another larger one of water; she also gave him a wallet full of provisions, and found him in much good meat. Moreover, she made the wind fair and warm for him, and gladly did Ulysses spread his sail before it, while he sat and guided the raft skilfully by means of the rudder. He never closed his eyes, but kept them fixed on the Pleiads, on late-setting Boötes, and on the Bear—which men also call the Wain, and which turns round and round where it is, facing Orion, and alone never dipping into the stream of Oceanus, for Calypso had told him to keep this to his left. Days seven and ten did he sail over the sea, and on the eighteenth the dim outlines of the mountains on the nearest part of the Phæacian coast appeared, rising like a shield on the horizon.

But King Neptune, who was returning from the Ethiopians, caught sight of Ulysses a long way off, from the mountains of the Solymi. He could see him sailing upon the sea, and it made him very angry, so he wagged his head and muttered to himself, saying, "Good heavens, so the gods have been changing their minds about Ulysses while I was away in Ethiopia, and now he is close to the land of the Phæacians, where it is decreed that he shall escape from the calamities that have befallen him. Still, he shall have plenty of hardship yet before he has done with it."

Thereon he gathered his clouds together, grasped his trident, stirred it round in the sea, and roused the rage of every wind that blows till earth, sea, and sky were hidden in cloud, and night sprang forth out of the heavens. Winds from East, South, North, and West fell upon him all at the same time, and a tremendous sea got up, so that Ulysses' heart began to fail him. "Alas," he said to himself in his dismay, "what ever will become of me? I am afraid Calypso was right when she said I should have trouble by sea before I got back home. It is all coming true. How black is Jove making heaven with his clouds, and what a sea the winds are raising from every quarter at once. I am now safe to perish. Blest and thrice blest were those Danaans who fell before Troy in the cause of the sons of Atreus. Would that I had been killed on the day when the Trojans were pressing me so sorely about the dead body of Achilles, for then I should have had due burial and the Achæans would have honoured my name; but now it seems that I shall come to a most pitiable end."

As he spoke a sea broke over him with such terrific fury that the raft reeled again, and he was carried overboard a long way off. He let go the helm, and the force of the hurricane was so great that it broke the mast half way up, and both sail and yard went over into the sea. For a long time Ulysses was under water, and it was all he could do to rise to the surface again, for the clothes Calypso had given him weighed him down; but at last he got his head above water and spat out the bitter brine that was running down his face in streams. In spite of all this, however, he did not lose sight of his raft, but swam as fast as he could towards it, got hold of it, and climbed on board again so as to escape drowning. The sea took the raft and tossed it about as autumn winds whirl thistledown round and round upon a road. It was as though the South, North, East, and West winds were all playing battledore and shuttlecock with it at once.

When he was in this plight, Ino daughter of Cadmus, also called Leucothea, saw him. She had formerly been a mere mortal, but had been since raised to the rank of a marine goddess. Seeing in what great distress Ulysses now was, she had compassion upon him, and, rising like a sea-gull from the waves, took her seat upon the raft.

"My poor good man," said she, "why is Neptune so furiously angry with you? He is giving you a great deal of trouble, but for all his bluster he will not kill you. You seem to be a sensible person, do then as I bid you; strip, leave your raft to drive before the wind, and swim to the Phæacian coast where better luck awaits you. And here, take my veil and put it round your chest; it is enchanted, and you can come to no harm so long as you wear it. As soon as you touch land take it off, throw it back as far as you can into the sea, and then go away again." With these words she took off her veil and gave it him. Then she dived down again like a sea-gull and vanished beneath the dark blue waters.

But Ulysses did not know what to think. "Alas," he said to himself in his dismay, "this is only some one or other of the gods who is luring me to ruin by advising me to quit my raft. At any rate I will not do so at present, for the land where she said I should be quit of all my troubles seemed to be still a good way off. I know what I will do—I am sure it will be best—no matter what happens I will stick to the raft as long as her timbers hold together, but when the sea breaks her up I will swim for it; I do not see how I can do any better than this."

While he was thus in two minds, Neptune sent a terrible great wave that seemed to rear itself above his head till it broke right over the raft, which then went to pieces as though it were a heap of dry chaff tossed about by a whirlwind. Ulysses got astride of one plank and rode upon it as if he were on horseback; he then took off the clothes Calypso had given him, bound Ino's veil under his arms, and plunged into the sea—meaning to swim on shore. King Neptune watched him as he did so, and wagged his head, muttering to himself and saying, "There now, swim up and down as you best can till you fall in with well-to-do people. I do not think you will be able to say that I have let you off too lightly." On this he lashed his horses and drove to Ægæ where his palace is.

But Minerva resolved to help Ulysses, so she bound the ways of all the winds except one, and made them lie quite still; but she roused a good stiff breeze from the North that should lay the waters till Ulysses reached the land of the Phæacians where he would be safe.

Thereon he floated about for two nights and two days in the water, with a heavy swell on the sea and death staring him in the face; but when the third day broke, the wind fell and there was a dead calm without so much as a breath of air stirring. As he rose on the swell he looked eagerly ahead, and could see land quite near. Then, as children rejoice when their dear father begins to get better after having for a long time borne sore affliction sent him by some angry spirit, but the gods deliver him from evil, so was Ulysses thankful when he again saw land and trees, and swam on with all his strength that he might once more set foot upon dry ground. When, however, he got within earshot, he began to hear the surf thundering up against the rocks, for the swell still broke against them with a terrific roar. Everything was enveloped in spray; there were no harbours where a ship might ride, nor shelter of any kind, but only headlands, low lying rocks, and mountain tops.

Ulysses' heart now began to fail him, and he said despairingly to himself, "Alas, Jove has let me see land after swimming so far that I had given up all hope, but I can find no landing place, for the coast is rocky and surf-beaten, the rocks are smooth and rise sheer from the sea, with deep water close under them so that I cannot climb out for want of foot hold. I am afraid some great wave will lift me off my legs and dash me against the rocks as I leave the water —which would give me a sorry landing. If, on the other hand, I swim further in search of some shelving beach or harbour, a hurricane may carry me out to sea again sorely against my will, or heaven may send some great monster of the deep to attack me; for Amphitrite breeds many such, and I know that Neptune is very angry with me."

While he was thus in two minds a wave caught him and took him with such force against the rocks that he would have been smashed and torn to pieces if Minerva had not shewn him what to do. He caught hold of the rock with both hands and clung to it groaning with pain till the wave retired, so he was saved that time; but presently the wave came on again and carried him back with it far into the sea —tearing his hands as the suckers of a polypus are torn when some one plucks it from its bed, and the stones come up along with it—even so did the rocks tear the skin from his strong hands, and then the wave drew him deep down under the water.

Here poor Ulysses would have certainly perished even in spite of his own destiny, if Minerva had not helped him to keep his wits about him. He swam seaward again, beyond reach of the surf that was beating against the land, and at the same time he kept looking towards the shore to see if he could find some haven, or a spit that should take the waves aslant. By and by, as he swam on, he came to the mouth of a river, and here he thought would be the best place, for there were no rocks, and it afforded shelter from the wind. He felt that there was a current, so he prayed inwardly and said:—

"Hear me, O king, whoever you may be, and save me from the anger of the sea-god Neptune, for I approach you prayerfully. Any one who has lost his way has at all times a claim even upon the gods, wherefore in my distress I draw near to your stream, and cling to the knees of your river-hood. Have mercy upon me O king, for I declare myself your suppliant."

Then the god staid his stream and stilled the waves, making all calm before him, and bringing him safely into the mouth of the river. Here at last Ulysses' knees and strong hands failed him, for the sea had completely broken him. His body was all swollen, and his mouth and nostrils ran down like a river with sea-water, so that he could neither breathe nor speak, and lay swooning from sheer exhaustion; presently, when he had got his breath and came to himself again, he took off the scarf that Ino had given him and threw it back into the salt stream of the river, whereon Ino received it into her hands from the wave that bore it towards her. Then he left the river, laid himself down among the rushes, and kissed the bounteous earth.

"Alas," he cried to himself in his dismay, "what ever will become of me, and how is it all to end? If I stay here upon the river bed through the long watches of the night, I am so exhausted that the bitter cold and damp may make an end of me—for towards sunrise there will be a keen wind blowing from off the river. If, on the other hand, I climb the hill side, find shelter in the woods, and sleep in some thicket, I may escape the cold and have a good night's rest, but some savage beast may take advantage of me and devour me."

In the end he deemed it best to take to the woods, and he found one upon some high ground not far from the water. There he crept beneath two shoots of olive that grew from a single stock—the one an ungrafted sucker, while the other had been grafted. No wind, however squally, could break through the cover they afforded, nor could the sun's rays pierce them, nor the rain get through them, so closely did they grow into one another. Ulysses crept under these and began to make himself a bed to lie on, for there was a great litter of dead leaves lying about—enough to make a covering for two or three men even in hard winter weather. He was glad enough to see this, so he laid himself down and heaped the leaves all round him. Then, as one who lives alone in the country, far from any neighbour, hides a brand as fire-seed in the ashes to save himself from having to get a light elsewhere, even so did Ulysses cover himself up with leaves; and Minerva shed a sweet sleep upon his eyes, closed his eyelids, and made him lose all memory of his sorrows.

So here Ulysses slept, overcome by sleep and toil; but

Minerva went off to the country and city of the Phæacians
—a people who used to live in the fair town of Hypereia,
near the lawless Cyclopes. Now the Cyclopes were
stronger than they and plundered them, so their king Nau-
sithous moved them thence and settled them in Scheria, far
from all other people. He surrounded the city with a wall,
built houses and temples, and divided the lands among his
people; but he was dead and gone to the house of Hades,
and King Alcinous, whose counsels were inspired of heaven, was now reigning. To his house, then, did Minerva
hie in furtherance of the return of Ulysses.

She went straight to the beautifully decorated bedroom
in which there slept a girl who was as lovely as a goddess,
Nausicaa, daughter to King Alcinous. Two maid servants
were sleeping near her, both very pretty, one on either side
of the doorway, which was closed with well made folding
doors. Minerva took the form of the famous sea captain
Dymas' daughter, who was a bosom friend of Nausicaa and
just her own age; then, coming up to the girl's bedside like
a breath of wind, she hovered over her head and said:—

"Nausicaa, what can your mother have been about, to
have such a lazy daughter? Here are your clothes all lying
in disorder, yet you are going to be married almost immediately, and should not only be well dressed yourself, but
should find good clothes for those who attend you. This is
the way to get yourself a good name, and to make your
father and mother proud of you. Suppose, then, that we
make tomorrow a washing day, and start at daybreak. I will
come and help you so that you may have everything ready
as soon as possible, for all the best young men among your
own people are courting you, and you are not going to
remain a maid much longer. Ask your father, therefore, to
have a waggon and mules ready for us at daybreak, to take

the rugs, robes, and girdles, and you can ride, too, which will be much pleasanter for you than walking, for the washing cisterns are some way from the town."

When she had said this Minerva went away to Olympus, which they say is the everlasting home of the gods. Here no wind beats roughly, and neither rain nor snow can fall; but it abides in everlasting sunshine and in a great peacefulness of light, wherein the blessed gods are illumined for ever and ever. This was the place to which the goddess went when she had given instructions to the girl.

By and by morning came and woke Nausicaa, who began wondering about her dream; she therefore went to the other end of the house to tell her father and mother all about it, and found them in their own room. Her mother was sitting by the fireside spinning her purple yarn with her maids around her, and she happened to catch her father just as he was going out to attend a meeting of the town council, which the Phæacian aldermen had convened. She stopped him and said:—

"Papa dear, could you manage to let me have a good big waggon? I want to take all our dirty clothes to the river and wash them. You are the chief man here, so it is only right that you should have a clean shirt when you attend meetings of the council. Moreover, you have five sons at home, two of them married, while the other three are good looking bachelors; you know they always like to have clean linen when they go to a dance, and I have been thinking about all this."

She did not say a word about her own wedding, for she did not like to, but her father knew and said, "You shall have the mules, my love, and whatever else you have a mind for. Be off with you, and the men shall get you a good strong waggon with a body to it that will hold all your clothes."

On this he gave his orders to the servants, who got the waggon out, harnessed the mules, and put them to, while the girl brought the clothes down from the linen room and placed them on the waggon. Her mother prepared her a basket of provisions with all sorts of good things, and a goat skin full of wine; the girl now got into the waggon, and her mother gave her also a golden cruse of oil, that she and her women might anoint themselves. Then she took the whip and reins and lashed the mules on, whereon they set off, and their hoofs clattered on the road. They pulled without flagging, and carried not only Nausicaa and her wash of clothes, but the maids also who were with her.

When they reached the water side they went to the washing cisterns, through which there ran at all times enough pure water to wash any quantity of linen, no matter how dirty. Here they unharnessed the mules and turned them out to feed on the sweet juicy herbage that grew by the water side. They took the clothes out of the waggon, put them in the water, and vied with one another in treading them in the pits to get the dirt out. After they had washed them and got them quite clean, they laid them out by the sea side, where the waves had raised a high beach of shingle, and set about washing themselves and anointing themselves with olive oil. Then they got their dinner by the side of the stream, and waited for the sun to finish drying the clothes. When they had done dinner they threw off the veils that covered their heads and began to play at ball, while Nausicaa sang for them. As the huntress Diana goes forth upon the mountains of Taÿgetus or Erymanthus to hunt wild boars or deer, and the wood nymphs, daughters of Ægis-bearing Jove, take their sport along with her (then is Leto proud at seeing her daughter stand a full head taller than the others, and eclipse the loveliest amid a whole bevy of beauties), even so did the girl outshine her handmaids.

When it was time for them to start home, and they were folding the clothes and putting them into the waggon, Minerva began to consider how Ulysses should wake up and see the handsome girl who was to conduct him to the city of the Phæacians. The girl, therefore, threw a ball at one of the maids, which missed her and fell into deep water. On this they all shouted, and the noise they made woke Ulysses, who sat up in his bed of leaves and began to wonder what it might all be.

"Alas," said he to himself, "what kind of people have I come amongst? Are they cruel, savage, and uncivilized, or hospitable and humane? I seem to hear the voices of young women, and they sound like those of the nymphs that haunt mountain tops, or springs of rivers and meadows of green grass. At any rate I am among a race of men and women. Let me try if I cannot manage to get a look at them."

As he said this he crept from under his bush, and broke off a bough covered with thick leaves to hide his nakedness. He looked like some lion of the wilderness that stalks about exulting in his strength and defying both wind and rain; his eyes glare as he prowls in quest of oxen, sheep, or deer, for he is famished, and will dare break even into a well fenced homestead, trying to get at the sheep—even such did Ulysses seem to the young women, as he drew near to them all naked as he was, for he was in great want. On seeing one so unkempt and so begrimed with salt water, the others scampered off along the spits that jutted out into the sea, but the daughter of Alcinous stood firm, for Minerva put courage into her heart and took away all fear from her. She stood right in front of Ulysses, and he doubted whether he should go up to her, throw himself at her feet, and embrace her knees as a suppliant, or stay where he was and entreat her to give him some clothes and show him the way to the town. In the end he deemed it best to entreat her from a distance in case the girl should take offence at his coming near enough to clasp her knees, so he addressed her in honeyed and persuasive language.

"Oh queen," he said, "I implore your aid—but tell me, are you a goddess or are you a mortal woman? If you are a goddess and dwell in heaven, I can only conjecture that you are Jove's daughter Diana, for your face and figure resemble none but hers; if on the other hand you are a mortal and live on earth, thrice happy are your father and mother—thrice happy, too, are your brothers and sisters; how proud and delighted they must feel when they see so fair a scion as yourself going out to a dance; most happy, however, of all will he be whose wedding gifts have been the richest, and who takes you to his own home. I never yet saw any one so beautiful, neither man nor woman, and am lost in admiration as I behold you. I can only compare you to a young palm tree which I saw when I was at Delos growing near the altar of Apollo—for I was there, too, with much people after me, when I was on that journey which has been the source of all my troubles. Never yet did such a young plant shoot out of the ground as that was, and I admired and wondered at it exactly as I now admire and wonder at yourself. I dare not clasp your knees, but I am in great distress; yesterday made the twentieth day that I have been tossing about upon the sea. The winds and waves have taken me all the way from the Ogygian island, and now fate has flung me upon this coast that I may endure still further suffering; for I do not think that I have yet come to the end of it, but rather that heaven has still much evil in store for me.

"And now, oh queen, have pity upon me, for you are the first person I have met, and I know no one else in this country. Show me the way to your town, and let me have anything that you may have brought hither to wrap your clothes in. May heaven grant you in all things your heart's desire—husband, house, and a happy, peaceful home; for there is nothing better in this world than that man and wife should be of one mind in a house. It discomfits their enemies, makes the hearts of their friends glad, and they themselves know more about it than any one."

To this Nausicaa answered, "Stranger, you appear to be a sensible well-disposed person. There is no accounting for luck; Jove gives prosperity to rich and poor just as he chooses, so you must take what he has seen fit to send you, and make the best of it. Now, however, that you have come to this our country, you shall not want for clothes nor for anything else that a foreigner in distress may reasonably look for. I will show you the way to the town, and will tell you the name of our people; we are called Phæacians, and I am daughter to Alcinous, in whom the whole power of the state is vested."

Then she called her maids and said, "Stay where you are, you girls. Can you not see a man without running away from him? Do you take him for a robber or a murderer? Neither he nor any one else can come here to do us Phæacians any harm, for we are dear to the gods, and live apart on a land's end that juts into the sounding sea, and have nothing to do with any other people. This is only some poor man who has lost his way, and we must be kind to him, for strangers and foreigners in distress are under Jove's protection, and will take what they can get and be thankful; so, girls, give the poor fellow something to eat and drink, and wash him in the stream at some place that is sheltered from the wind."

On this the maids left off running away and began calling one another back. They made Ulysses sit down in the shelter as Nausicaa had told them, and brought him a shirt and cloak. They also brought him the little golden cruse of oil, and told him to go and wash in the stream. But Ulysses said, "Young women, please to stand a little on one side that I may wash the brine from my shoulders and anoint myself with oil, for it is long enough since my skin has had a drop of oil upon it. I cannot wash as long as you all keep standing there. I am ashamed to strip before a number of good looking young women."

Then they stood on one side and went to tell the girl, while Ulysses washed himself in the stream and scrubbed the brine from his back and from his broad shoulders. When he had thoroughly washed himself, and had got the brine out of his hair, he anointed himself with oil, and put on the clothes which the girl had given him; Minerva then made him look taller and stronger than before, she also made the hair grow thick on the top of his head, and flow down in curls like hyacinth blossoms; she glorified him about the head and shoulders as a skilful workman who has studied art of all kinds under Vulcan and Minerva enriches a piece of silver plate by gilding it—and his work is full of beauty. Then he went and sat down a little way off upon the beach, looking quite young and handsome, and the girl gazed on him with admiration; then she said to her maids:—

"Hush, my dears, for I want to say something. I believe the gods who live in heaven have sent this man to the Phæacians. When I first saw him I thought him plain, but now his appearance is like that of the gods who dwell in heaven. I should like my future husband to be just such another as he is, if he would only stay here and not want to go away. However, give him something to eat and drink."

They did as they were told, and set food before Ulysses, who ate and drank ravenously, for it was long since he had had food of any kind. Meanwhile, Nausicaa bethought her of another matter. She got the linen folded and placed in the waggon, she then yoked the mules, and, as she took her seat, she called Ulysses:

"Stranger," said she, "rise and let us be going back to the town; I will introduce you at the house of my excellent father, where I can tell you that you will meet all the best people among the Phæacians. But be sure and do as I bid you, for you seem to be a sensible person. As long as we are going past the fields and farm lands, follow briskly behind the waggon along with the maids and I will lead the way myself. Presently, however, we shall come to the town, where you will find a high wall running all round it, and a good harbour on either side with a narrow entrance into the city, and the ships will be drawn up by the road side, for every one has a place where his own ship can lie. You will see the market place with a temple of Neptune in the middle of it, and paved with large stones bedded in the earth. Here people deal in ship's gear of all kinds, such as cables and sails, and here, too, are the places where oars are made, for the Phæacians are not a nation of archers; they know nothing about bows and arrows, but are a sea-faring folk, and pride themselves on their masts, oars, and ships, with which they travel far over the sea.

"I am afraid of the gossip and scandal that may be set on foot against me later on; for the people here are very ill-natured, and some low fellow, if he met us, might say,

'Who is this fine looking stranger that is going about with Nausicaa? Where did she find him? I suppose she is going to marry him. Perhaps he is a vagabond sailor whom she has taken from some foreign vessel, for we have no neighbours; or some god has at last come down from heaven in answer to her prayers, and she is going to live with him all the rest of her life. It would be a good thing if she would take herself off and find a husband somewhere else, for she will not look at one of the many excellent young Phæacians who are in love with her.' This is the kind of disparaging remark that would be made about me, and I could not complain, for I should myself be scandalised at seeing any other girl do the like, and go about with men in spite of everybody, while her father and mother were still alive, and without having been married in the face of all the world.

"If, therefore, you want my father to give you an escort and to help you home, do as I bid you; you will see a beautiful grove of poplars by the road side dedicated to Minerva; it has a well in it and a meadow all round it. Here my father has a field of rich garden ground, about as far from the town as a man's voice will carry. Sit down there and wait for a while till the rest of us can get into the town and reach my father's house. Then, when you think we must have done this, come into the town and ask the way to the house of my father Alcinous. You will have no difficulty in finding it; any child will point it out to you, for no one else in the whole town has anything like such a fine house as he has. When you have got past the gates and through the outer court, go right across the inner court till you come to my mother. You will find her sitting by the fire and spinning her purple wool by firelight. It is a fine sight to see her as she leans back against one of the bearing-posts with her maids all ranged behind her. Close to her seat stands that of my father, on which he sits and topes like an immortal god. Never mind him, but go up to my mother, and lay your hands upon her knees if you would get home quickly. If you can gain her over, you may hope to see your own country again, no matter how distant it may be."

So saying she lashed the mules with her whip and they left the river. The mules drew well, and their hoofs went up and down upon the road. She was careful not to go too fast for Ulysses and the maids who were following on foot along with the waggon, so she plied her whip with judgement. As the sun was going down they came to the sacred grove of Minerva, and there Ulysses sat down and prayed to the mighty daughter of Jove.

"Hear me," he cried, "daughter of Ægis-bearing Jove, unweariable, hear me now, for you gave no heed to my prayers when Neptune was wrecking me. Now, therefore, have pity upon me and grant that I may find friends and be hospitably received by the Phæacians."

Thus did he pray, and Minerva heard his prayer, but she would not show herself to him openly, for she was afraid of her uncle Neptune, who was still furious in his endeavours to prevent Ulysses from getting home.

RHAMPSINITUS AND
THE ROBBERS

BY HERODOTUS

Herodotus was born in Halicarnassus, in Asia Minor, about
485 B.C., and died in 425 or thereabouts. His great book, *The
Histories*, records the long hostility of Persia and the Greeks,
culminating with Xerxes' unsuccessful invasion of Greece in
480. In his efforts to obtain eye-witness reports and local color
Herodotus visited the countries of which he wrote, including
Egypt, Mesopotamia, Palestine, and the Ukraine. He was an
honest historian and a scrupulous reporter; his work may be
regarded as journalism of the highest order. He could never
resist a good story, though he might retell it with a gently
skeptical smile.

These translations of four stories are by Morris Bishop. The
first is from Book II, sections 121–122.

W HEN KING PROTEUS of Egypt died he was succeeded,
I was told, by Rhampsinitus. The story goes that he
possessed a great quantity of bullion, so much, in fact, that
hardly any of the succeeding Pharaohs surpassed or even
approached his wealth. To keep his treasure secure he had a
great stone stronghold built within his palace, against an
exterior wall. But the builder, who clearly had nefarious
designs, so disposed things that he left one of the stones
unmortared, easily removable by two men, or even by one
alone. The strongroom was completed, and the king stored
there his wealth.

Well, time marched on; the builder felt his end approaching. He summoned his two sons, and told them that
to provide for them and enable them to live in affluence he
had made his little contrivance in the king's treasure-room.

He explained everything clearly, the measurements for locating the stone and the mode of removing it, and told how, if they followed directions, they would be the effective Comptrollers of the Treasury. He then died. His sons lost no time in setting to work. They went to the palace by night, found the stone in the outer wall, readily worked it out, and purloined a good load of silver.

The next time the king inspected the quarters, he was amazed to observe that the level of money in some containers had sunk. He could not imagine whom to accuse. The seals and locks of the strongroom were intact. On two or three later visits it appeared that more money was missing (for in fact the thieves kept right on with their depredations). He decided then to have some man-traps made, and set them near the vessels containing his stores of money. This done, in due course the burglars paid their visit. One of them, making straight for the money-jars, was caught and held fast. Well aware of his predicament, he immediately called to his brother, told him what had happened, and bade the brother enter with all speed and cut off his head, so that when his body was discovered it would not be recognized, to the destruction of both of them. The other realized that this course was the only sensible one. He followed instructions, and, carrying his brother's head, replaced the stone and made off for home.

Early next morning the king entered the strongroom and was astounded on finding the body of the thief in the trap, lacking a head, while the room was intact, showing no signs of human entry or exit. After reflection, he gave orders that the thief's body should be hung on the outer wall, and that guards should be detailed to watch it, and if any persons should be observed lamenting there they should be seized and brought to the king's presence.

When the youths' mother heard the terrible news of her

son's death and of the exposure of his corpse, she upbraided her surviving son, and commanded him to recover somehow his brother's body. She threatened that if he should fail to do so she would go to the king and denounce him as the thief. She reviled him with many bitter words; he protested but could not change her mind.

Finally he settled on this scheme: he filled some skins with wine, loaded them on donkeys' backs, and drove the steeds before him. When they passed before the guards of the dead body he untied the lashings of two or three spouts of the dependent wine-skins. The wine dribbled down; he beat his head and shouted, as if too dazed to decide which of the skins to tend to first. When the guards saw the wine flowing free they were delighted by the bit of luck; they grabbed receptacles and ran out into the road to catch the bounty. The driver yelled at them in pretended anger; the guards tried to console him. He appeared to calm down and make the best of things. He drove his asses off the road and set to repacking them. There was much joking and joshing; one of the soldiers made the driver laugh, whereupon he presented them with one of his wine-skins. Then they decided to sit down where they were and make a binge of it, and they urged their kind friend to join in. He let himself be persuaded, and joined the party. As they drank and drank and became the fastest of friends, the donkey-driver presented them with another wine-skin. At length, overcome with drink, the guards all collapsed and ere long were fast bound in drunken slumber. The thief waited till night was well advanced, then took down his brother's body. Then, in derision, he clipped off the right side of all the soldiers' beards, and so left them. He placed the corpse on the back of one of his asses and brought it back to his mother, as he had promised.

When the theft of the dead thief was reported to the

king, he was furious indeed. Wishing to capture the trickster at any cost, he contrived a trick of his own (which I personally find hard to credit). He installed his own daughter in a bawdy-house, ordering her to welcome all customers alike, but before proceeding to business to require of each one to tell her what were the wickedest and the cleverest things he had done in his life. And if anyone should tell her the story of the stolen thief, she was to seize him and not let him go. The daughter obeyed her father's commands. But the thief, divining the king's purpose, wished to outdo him in cleverness. He got possession of a corpse freshly dead, cut off the arm at the shoulder, hid the arm under his cloak, and paid a visit to the king's daughter. When she put the usual question to him, he replied that the wickedest thing he had ever done was to cut off the head of his brother, who was caught in a trap in the king's treasury; and the cleverest thing was to get the guards drunk and cut down his brother's gibbeted body. When the girl heard this she grabbed at him; but, in the dark, the thief held out to her the dead man's arm. She seized it, thinking it to be his own. The thief left it with her and escaped through the door.

When word of this was brought to the king, he was astonished at the man's smartness and boldness. Finally he had announcements made in all his cities of a free pardon for the culprit and a great reward, if he should make himself known. The thief confidently appeared before Rhampsinitus. The king marvelled at him, regarding him as the most brilliant of men, and thus gave him his daughter's hand in marriage. "The Egyptians," he said, "are the cleverest men in the world, and this fellow is the cleverest of the Egyptians."

THE RING OF
POLYCRATES
BY HERODOTUS

This translation, by Morris Bishop, is from Book III, sections
39–43, of *The Histories.*

POLYCRATES, son of Aeaces, gained mastery of the island
of Samos in a revolution. At first he divided the little
state into three parts, sharing the rule with his brothers
Pantagnotus and Syloson. Later, however, he put the elder,
Pantagnotus, to death and banished Syloson. Thus he held
the whole island of Samos. Then he made a pact of friendship with Amasis, king of Egypt, with an exchange of gifts.
Before long his power increased so far that all Ionia and
Greece were aware of it. Wherever he made war success
awaited him. He had a hundred penteconters, fifty-oared
ships, and a force of a thousand archers. He fought everyone indiscriminately, for he maintained that he got more
gratitude for returning something to a defeated enemy than
for sparing him in the first place. He took many of the
islands, and also many cities on the Asian mainland. He
conquered the Lesbians, among others, in a great sea-battle.
They had come in full strength to the aid of Miletus. As
prisoners, they dug the moat around the Samos citadel.

King Amasis was well informed of Polycrates' remarkable good fortune and was much concerned by it. And as
success followed success, Amasis addressed the following
letter to him in Samos: "Amasis to Polycrates, greetings. It
is a great pleasure to learn that a friend and guest prospers.
But I am not entirely happy about your triumphs; for the

gods, I know, are jealous gods. What I most wish for myself and for those I love is a proper alternation of gains and losses, a life compounded of good fortune and ill, rather than unbroken success. I never yet heard of any constant winner who didn't finally land in calamity and ruin. So listen to me: break the run of good luck. Consider which of your possessions is most dear to you, which one you would be most sorry to lose. And throw it away, so that no man may ever see it again. And if after this you don't have some bad luck along with the good, repeat the process, and thus disarm fate."

Polycrates pondered the letter and recognized that Amasis' advice was sound. He considered which of his stored-up treasures he would be most afflicted to lose, and after much thought came to a decision. He wore a seal ring, an emerald set in gold, made by Theodorus, son of Telecles of Samos. He decided to throw this away. He ordered out a penteconter and put forth to the open sea. When he was far from the island he removed the ring, and, in the view of the whole crew, threw it into the sea. He then returned home, in a very sad state of mind.

Five or six days later it chanced that a fisherman caught a very big, fine fish, fit, he thought, only for the royal table. So he carried it to the palace door and asked to see the king. Polycrates had him admitted; whereupon he presented the fish, and said: "My lord the king, when I caught this fish I decided not to take it to market, although I am just a poor fisherman. I thought it was fit only for a king in his glory; and so I bring it to you as a present." The king was pleased by these words; he replied: "You did very well, my friend; I thank you for your words and for your gift; and I hope you will return and dine with me." Mightily proud, the fisherman went off to his home. And the servants, cutting up the fish, found Polycrates' signet ring in its belly. They plucked it out and brought it, rejoicing, to Polycrates, and told him how they had found it. He recognized the workings of fate; he wrote a letter describing the event and his own actions, and sent it off to King Amasis in Egypt.

When Amasis read Polycrates' letter, he realized that no one man can save another from the destiny decreed for him, and that as Polycrates' luck held so far that he even found what he threw away, he was bound to come to a bad end. He therefore sent an envoy to Samos to break off their friendly alliance, so that, when the inevitable calamity should arrive, he would not be bound to painful sympathy.

[Polycrates was in fact lured to his death by an enemy, and was slain "in a mode which is not fit to be described." His body was crucified.]

ZOPYRUS, THE
DOUBLE AGENT
BY HERODOTUS

This translation, by Morris Bishop, is from Book III, sections 150–160, of *The Histories.*

AFTER THE Persian fleet had sailed for Samos, the Babylonians revolted. They had made long and careful preparations while the city was in upheaval; and somehow or other they had kept their arrangements secret. When the time came for the outbreak, this was their procedure: they sent away all the mothers, then each man picked one woman from his household, anyone he pleased, to be the breadmaker. The other women were all gathered together and strangled, so that they would not waste the food supplies.

When the news reached King Darius, he assembled all his forces, marched to Babylon and besieged it. But little the Babylonians cared. They manned the battlements of their walls and shouted abuse at Darius and his army. One man cried: "What are you sitting there for, Persians? You might as well go away. Sure you will take our city—when mules bear foals!" This Babylonian presumed that never would a mule bear offspring.

A year and seven months went by. Darius and his whole army were furious, being forever balked by the Babylonian defense. He tried every trick in the book, including the device by which Cyrus had taken the city, long before. It was no use. The Babylonians were always on the watch, and Darius could find no way to take them.

At last, in the twentieth month, a remarkable thing happened to Zopyrus, son of that Megabyzus who was one of the seven men who overthrew the Magus. One of his pack-mules dropped a foal! Zopyrus refused to believe the report; but when he saw the foal with his own eyes he ordered those who had seen it to keep quiet. He recollected the jeer of the Babylonian at the beginning of the siege: "You will take our city when mules bear foals!" Reflecting on these words, he thought that Babylon might now be taken, for he thought he recognized divine intention in the man's words and the foaling of his own mule.

Being then convinced that Babylon was doomed, he called upon Darius and asked whether he really regarded the capture of the city as all-important. On the king's assurance that indeed he did so, Zopyrus meditated on how he might compass the city's fall and gain full credit for it. (Among the Persians spectacular deeds are highly honored and well rewarded.) He could think of no better way to reduce the city than to mutilate himself and in this state to go over, apparently, to the enemy. He accepted the necessity of doing himself permanent injury. He cut off his nose and his ears, shaved his head close, and lashed his own back; and in this guise he presented himself before Darius.

The king was shocked at the sight of a high noble so maimed. He sprang up from his throne with a cry and demanded to know who had thus mistreated Zopyrus and why. Said Zopyrus: "You, O king, are the only man on earth who could bring me to this pass. No one other than myself alone has thus disfigured me; for I could not bear that Assyrians should mock at Persians."

"My poor friend," said Darius, "your purpose may be noble, but your deed is folly, if you think that by mutilating yourself you can hasten the enemy's surrender! You were mad to inflict this horrid injury on yourself!"

"If I had told you what I had in mind," said Zopyrus,

"you would have forbidden it; so I took my own counsel and acted upon it. Now then, if you do your part properly, Babylon will be ours. I will desert into the city, all bloody as I am; and I will assert that you have done this to me. And I am sure I will convince them, and they will give me a high army post. And you do this: wait till the tenth day after I get into the city, and then post a thousand of the most expendable men in your army before what is called the Semiramis Gate. Then on the seventh day after that, put two thousand men before the Nineveh Gate. Wait another twenty days, and then station four thousand before the Chaldean Gate, as they call it. Don't equip these men —or those of the first detachment—with any weapons but their daggers; you can leave them these. When the twenty days are over, have the rest of the army deliver a mass assault on the whole circuit of the walls, and assign the elite Persian troops to the Belian and the Cissian gates. For I am sure that I shall so commend myself to the Babylonians that they will entrust everything to me, even the keys of their gates. Then it will be up to me and to the Persian soldiers to do the rest."

After leaving these instructions, Zopyrus stole toward the city gate, glancing fearfully back like a genuine deserter. When the sentinels on the towers saw him they ran down, opened the gate a crack, and asked him who he was and what he was doing there. He told them that he was Zopyrus and that he was defecting to them. The sentinels, on hearing this, brought him forthwith before the Babylonian council. In its presence he indicated his wretched state, blaming Darius for his mistreatment, only because he had advised the king to raise the siege, since there appeared to be no hope of taking the city. He said: "Now, O Babylonians, I bring to you the greatest of gifts, and to Darius and his Persian army the greatest evil. He shall not escape scot-free for his outrageous treatment of me. For I know all his purposes and plans."

When the Babylonians saw this most eminent Persian with his nose and ears cut off and with his body covered with bloody welts they had no doubt that he was telling the truth and that he had come over to their side. They readily granted his request for the command of an army. When this was entrusted to him he acted as he had planned with Darius. On the tenth day after his flight he led out his Babylonian army and surrounded and annihilated the first thousand Persians whom Darius had sent out to be sacrificed. Seeing that his actions matched his words, the Babylonians were mightily pleased, and were ready to do anything he might ask. When the agreed number of days had passed he led out a picked body of Babylonian troops and utterly destroyed the two thousand men of Darius' army. At this second triumph the Babylonians treated Zopyrus as a popular hero. Then, the stipulated time having arrived, he issued forth to the place agreed upon, surrounded there the four thousand, and slaughtered them all. After this feat Zopyrus was the city's darling; he was made commanding general and custodian of the defenses.

Then Darius, according to the plan, delivered a general attack on the whole circuit of the walls. And then Zopyrus revealed himself in his true colors. While the Babylonians manned the walls to resist the assault, he threw open the Cissian and Belian gates and admitted the Persian host. Those Babylonians who saw his action took refuge in the temple of Jupiter Belus, but most, unaware, remained at their posts until they learned too late that they had been betrayed.

Thus was Babylon taken for the second time. Darius, the victor, breached the walls and removed the gates. (Cyrus had neglected to do so at his conquest.) He then impaled about three thousand of the prominent citizens; the rest he allowed to remain in the city. Further, to keep the Babylonians' stock from dying out (for, as I said before, they had strangled most of their women to economize provisions), he drafted a fixed proportion of women from the neighboring nations. No less than fifty thousand women were thus collected. These were the mothers of the present Babylonians.

In Darius' opinion Zopyrus was the greatest servant of the Persian state who had ever lived, excepting only Cyrus, with whom no Persian would venture to compare anyone. It is said that Darius often declared that he would rather have had Zopyrus whole and intact than twenty Babylons. He showered Zopyrus with honors, annually presenting him with gifts such as are most prized among the Persians. Also he made Zopyrus governor for life of Babylon, with exemption from taxes; and he did much else besides.

THE WOOING
OF AGARISTA
BY HERODOTUS

This translation, by Morris Bishop, is from Book VI, sections
125–129, of *The Histories*.

THE ALCMAEONIDAE were a very distinguished family in
Athens from the earliest times, and later during the life
of Alcmaeon and Megacles after him they became very
prominent. When Croesus sent his Lydians from Sardis to
consult the Delphic oracle, Alcmaeon gave the envoys
every assistance. Croesus, hearing from his messengers of
Alcmaeon's kindnesses, invited him to Sardis, and on his
arrival offered him as much gold as he could carry on his
person. Alcmaeon made due preparations; he put on a flowing tunic, which he could hold out in front like an apron,
and a pair of enormous open-top boots; and thus he followed his guides into the treasure-house. Attacking a
mound of gold-dust, he packed into his top-boots as much
as they would hold; then he filled the concavity of his tunic
with gold, powdered his hair with gold-dust, and took a
good mouthful of it. Then, barely able to walk, he tottered
out like something hardly human, with his mouth and body
all puffed out with gold. When Croesus saw him he roared
with laughter, and told him to keep all his cargo and indeed
to double it. Thus Alcmaeon's family became very rich,
and he was able to support four-horsed chariots, with
which he won the races at Olympia.

In the next generation Cleisthenes, despot of Sicyon,
made his family even more eminent than before, so that it

was renowned throughout Greece. He had a daughter named Agarista; he wanted to marry her to the best man in all Greece. Therefore, after he had won the chariot-race at Olympia, he made a public announcement: "Whatever Greek thinks himself worthy to be Cleisthenes' son-in-law may present himself within sixty days in Sicyon; and in a year from that time Cleisthenes will choose a mate for his daughter."

All the Greeks who had a high opinion of themselves or of their cities flocked to Sicyon to enter the lists. Cleisthenes had a running-track and a wrestling-floor specially made for their trials. From Italy came Smindyrides of Sybaris, son of Hippocrates. (Sybaris was then at the height of its fame.) Smindyrides was famed for the sumptuous elegance of his life. From Siris, also in Italy, came Damasus, son of Amyris called the Wise. From the Ionian Gulf was Amphimnestus of Epidamnus, son of Epistrophus. Males came from Aetolia; he was the brother of that Titormus, the strongest man in Greece, who took such a dislike to humanity that he retired to the remotest part of Aetolia. There were several from the Peloponnesus, notably Leocedes, son of Pheidon, king of Argos, who introduced a system of weights and measures to the Peloponnesus, and who committed the most dastardly act ever done by a Greek—he ousted the Elean managers of the Olympic games and ran them himself. . . . Athens sent two contestants: Megacles, son of the Alcmaeon who visited Croesus, and Hippocleides, son of Tisandrus, the richest and handsomest man in Athens. . . .

Such was the roll of the suitors. On the appointed day Cleisthenes examined each of them on his country and background. Then he made trial of them all, testing their manly spirit and temper, their character and accomplishments, sometimes in tête-à-tête and sometimes in groups. He made the younger ones work out in the gymnasium. But the severest test was of their behavior at the dinner-table. During their whole stay he supplied all their wants and always entertained them magnificently. The two candidates he liked best were the Athenians, and of the two he inclined toward Hippocleides, son of Tisandrus, both because of his manly virtues and because he was related to the Cypselid family of Corinth.

At length the fated day of the betrothal announcement arrived; Cleisthenes had to publish his decision. He first sacrificed a hundred oxen, and then offered a great banquet to the suitors and all the people of Sicyon. After dinner the candidates displayed their skill in music and in improvised speech-making. As the wine flowed freely Hippocleides outshone all the rest. He called on the flute-player for more music; and as the flutist obliged, he danced to the tune, to his own great satisfaction. But Cleisthenes began to glower at the whole business. Then Hippocleides demanded that a table be brought in; he mounted it and performed Laconian dances and Attic figures. Then he stood on his head on the table and waved his legs about to music.

Now at the first and second rounds of dancing Cleisthenes had begun to entertain serious doubts about Hippocleides' fitness to be his son-in-law, but he contained himself, out of decency. However, when he saw the fellow gesticulating with his legs he could restrain himself no more; he cried: "Son of Tisandrus, you have danced away your wife!"

"I should worry!" was Hippocleides' only reply.

The phrase has become a popular cliché.

THE EUBOEAN HUNTER
BY DIO CHRYSOSTOM

Dio Cocceianus, called Chrysostom, "golden-mouthed," for his eloquence, was born about A.D. 40 in Prusa, now the important Turkish city of Bursa, near the Hellespont. A too free-spoken cynic, he was banished in A.D. 82 and was obliged to put his philosophy to the test. Ragged and penniless, supporting himself sometimes by manual labor, but with Plato and Demosthenes always in pocket, he wandered about the Empire. Eventually he gained the favor of the Emperors Nerva and Trajan. He wrote abundantly, on philosophy, politics, and literature. He died in Prusa, at about eighty.

This translation is reprinted by permission of the publishers and THE LOEB CLASSICAL LIBRARY from J. W. Cohoon, translator, Dio Chrysostom, *Discourses*, Volume I (Cambridge, Mass.: Harvard University Press, 1932).

I SHALL NOW relate a personal experience of mine; not merely something I have heard from others. Perhaps, indeed, it is quite natural for an old man to be garrulous and reluctant to drop any subject that occurs to him, and possibly this is just as true of the wanderer as of the old man. The reason, I dare say, is that both have had many experiences that they find considerable pleasure in recalling. Anyhow I shall describe the character and manner of life of some people that I met in practically the centre of Greece.

It chanced that at the close of the summer season I was crossing from Chios with some fishermen in a very small boat, when such a storm arose that we had great difficulty in reaching the Hollows of Euboea * in safety. The crew

* The dangerous east coast of the southern part of Euboea, a large island off the east coast of mainland Greece.—Ed.

ran their boat up a rough beach under the cliffs, where it was wrecked, and then went off to a company of purple-fishers * whose vessel was anchored in the shelter of the spur of rocks near by, and they planned to stay there and work along with them. So I was left alone, and not know-ing of any town in which to seek shelter, I wandered aimlessly along the shore on the chance that I might find some boat sailing by or riding at anchor. I had gone on a considerable distance without seeing anybody when I chanced upon a deer that had just fallen over the cliff and lay in the wash of the breakers, lapped by the waves and still breathing. And soon I thought I heard the barking of dogs above, but not clearly, owing to the roar of the sea. On going forward and gaining an elevated position with great difficulty, I saw the dogs baffled, running to and fro, and inferred that their quarry, being hard pressed by them, had jumped over the cliff. Then, soon after, I saw a man, a hunter, to judge by his appearance and dress; he wore a beard on his healthy face, and not simply hair at the back of his head in mean and base fashion, as Homer says the Euboeans did when they went against Troy, mocking and ridiculing them, it seems to me, because, while the other Greeks there made a good appearance, they had hair on only half the head.

Now this man hailed me, saying, "Stranger, have you seen a deer running anywhere hereabouts?" And I replied, "Yonder it is this minute, in the surf," and I took him and showed it to him. So he dragged it out of the sea, ripped off the skin with his knife while I lent a helping hand as best I could. Then, after cutting off the hind quarters, he was about to carry them away along with the hide, when he

* Men who dredged up the shell-fish from which the purple dye, in fact dark red, was made.

invited me to come along and dine upon the venison with him, adding that his dwelling was not far away. "And then in the morning," he continued, "after you have rested with us, you shall come back to the sea, since the present is no weather for sailing. Yet do not worry about that," he continued, "I should be content to have the wind die down after full five days, but that is not likely when the peaks of the Euboean mountains are so capped with clouds as you see them now." And at the same time he asked me whence I came, how I had landed there, and whether the boat had not been wrecked. "It was a very small one," I replied, "belonging to some fishermen who were crossing over, and I, their only passenger, sailed with them on urgent business, but all the same it ran aground and was wrecked." "Well, it could not easily have been otherwise," he replied; "for see, how wild and rugged the part of the island is that faces the sea. These are what they call the Hollows of Euboea, where a ship is doomed if it is driven ashore, and rarely are any of those aboard saved either, unless, of course, like you they sail in a very light craft. But come and have no fear. Today you shall rest after your trying experience, but tomorrow we shall do our best to get you out safely, now that we have come to know you. You look to me like a man from the city, not a sailor or worker on the land, nay, you seem to be suffering from some grievous infirmity of body, to judge by your leanness."

I followed him gladly without fear of any treachery, since I had nothing but a shabby cloak. Now I had often found in other situations like this—for I was continually roaming about—and I certainly did in this one, that poverty is in reality a sacred and inviolable thing and no one wrongs you; yes, much less than they wrong those who carry the herald's wand. And so I followed without misgiving on this occasion. And it was about five miles to his place.

As we proceeded on our way he told me of his circumstances and how he lived with his wife and children. "There are two of us, stranger," he said, "who live in the same place. Each is married to a sister of the other, and we have children by them, sons and daughters. We live by the chase for the most part and work but a small bit of land. You see, the place does not belong to us: we did not inherit it or get it by our own efforts. Our fathers, though free, were just as poor as we are—hired herdsmen tending the cattle of a wealthy man, one of the residents of the island here, a man who owned many droves of horses and cattle, many flocks, many good fields too and many other possessions together with all these hills. Now when he died and his property was confiscated—they say he was put to death by the emperor * for his wealth—they at once drove off his stock to be butchered, and in addition to his stock our own few cattle, and, as for our wages, no one has ever paid them. At that time, then, we stayed of necessity at the place where we happened to have had our cattle and had built certain huts and an enclosure of palings for the calves, not very large or strong—just what would do for the summer, I suppose; for in the winter we grazed our cattle in the flat lands, where we had plenty of pasturage and a good deal of hay put up; but in the summer we would drive them into the hills. It was in this place especially that our fathers made their steadings; for the place sloped in from both sides, forming a ravine, deep and shaded; through the centre flowed a quiet stream in which the cows and calves could wade with perfect ease; the water was abundant and pure, bubbling up from a spring near by; and in the summer a

* Domitian.

breeze always blew through the ravine. Then the glades round about were soft and moist, breeding never a gadfly or any other cattle pest. Many very beautiful meadows stretched beneath tall sparse trees, and the whole district abounded in luxuriant vegetation throughout the entire summer, so that the cattle did not range very far. For these reasons they regularly established the herd there.

"Now our fathers remained in the huts at that time, hoping to hire out or find some work, and they lived on the produce of a very small piece of land which they happened to have under cultivation near the cattle-yard. This was quite enough for them as it was well manured. And having nothing more to do with cattle they turned to hunting, sometimes going alone and at other times with dogs; for two of those which had followed the cattle, after going a long distance and not seeing the herdsmen, had left the herd and returned to the place. These at first merely followed as if out for some other purpose than hunting, and though, when they saw wolves, they would give chase for a distance, yet to boars or deer they would pay no attention whatever. But whenever they sighted a bear, whether early or late, they would rally to the attack, barking and fending him off, as if they were fighting a man. And so, from tasting the blood of boars and deer and often eating their flesh, they changed their habits late in life and learned to like meat instead of barley-bread, gorging themselves with it whenever any game was caught and going hungry otherwise, till they finally gave more attention to the chase, pursued with equal zest every animal they sighted, began to pick up the scent and trails in some way or other, and thus changed from shepherd dogs into a sort of late-trained and rather slow hunting dogs.

"Then when winter came on, there was no work in sight for the men whether they came down to town or to a village. So after making their huts tighter and the yard fence closer, they managed to get along and worked the whole of that plot, and the winter hunting proved easier. The tracks were naturally clearer, because printed on the damp ground, and the snow made them visible at a great distance, so that there was no need of a troublesome search, since a high-road, as it were, led to them, and the quarry was sluggish and waited longer. It is possible, besides, to catch hares and gazelles in their lairs. In this way, then, our fathers lived from that time on, no longer having any desire for a different kind of life. And they married us their sons to wives, each giving his own daughter. The two old men died about a year ago, counting the many years they had lived, but being still strong and youthful and vigorous of body. Of the mothers mine is yet living.

"Now the other one of us has never yet been to town, though he is fifty years old, and I only twice—once when I was still a boy, with my father, when we had the cattle; and later on a man came demanding money, under the impression that we had some, and bade us follow him to the city. Now we had no money and swore on oath that we had not, adding that otherwise we would have given it. We entertained him as best we could and gave him two deerskins, and I followed him to the city; * for he said it was necessary for one of us to go and explain this matter.

"Now, as on my former trip, I saw many large houses and a strong surrounding wall with a number of lofty square structures † on the wall and many boats lying in complete calm at anchor in a lake as it were. There is nothing like that anywhere here where you put in, and that is why the ships are wrecked. Now that is what I saw, and a big crowd herded in together and a tremendous uproar and shouting, so that I thought they were all fighting with one

* Carystus or Chalcis is thought of.   † I.e., towers.

another. Well, he brought me before certain magistrates and said with a laugh, 'This is the man you sent me for. He has nothing but his long hair and a hut of very strong timber.' Then the officials went into the theatre * and I with them. The theatre is hollow like a ravine, except that it is not long in two directions but semicircular, and not natural but built of stone. But perhaps you are laughing at me for telling you what you know perfectly well.

"Now at first the crowd deliberated on other matters for a considerable while, and they kept up a shouting, at one time in gentle fashion and all of them in cheerful mood, as they applauded certain speakers, but at other times with vehemence and in wrath. This wrath of theirs was something terrible, and they at once frightened the men against whom they raised their voices, so that some of them ran about begging for mercy, while others threw off their cloaks through fear. I too myself was once almost knocked over by the shouting, as though a tidal wave or thunderstorm had suddenly broken over me. And other men would come forward, or stand up where they were, and address the multitude, sometimes using a few words, at other times making long speeches. To some of these they would listen for quite a long time, but at others they were angry as soon as they opened their mouths, and they would not let them so much as cheep.

"But when they finally settled down and there was quiet, they brought me forward. And someone cried out, 'This man, sirs, is one of the fellows who have been enjoying the use of our public land for many years, and not only he but his father before him. They graze their cattle on our mountains, farm and hunt, have built many houses, have set out vines, and enjoy many other advantages without paying

---

* Theatres were common all over Greece, and public meetings were generally held in them.

rent to anybody for the land or ever having received it from the people as a gift. For what, pray, would they ever have received it? And though they occupy what is ours and are wealthy, yet they have never performed any public service, nor do they pay any tax on what they make, but live free from taxes and public services as though they were benefactors of the city. Yes, and I believe,' he continued, 'that they have never come here before.' I shook my head, and the crowd laughed when they saw it. This laughing enraged the speaker and he abused me roundly. Then turning toward the audience once more, he said, 'Well, then, if these doings meet with your approval, we had all better lose no time in looting the public property, some of us taking the city's money, just as certain individuals are even now doing, no doubt, and others squatting upon the land without your consent, if you are going to let these backwoodsmen hold without payment more than 250 acres of the best land, from which you might get three Attic measures * of grain per head.'

"When I heard this, I laughed as loud as I could. The crowd, however, did not laugh as before but became very noisy, while the fellow grew angry, and giving me a fierce look, said, 'Do you see the deceitfulness and impudence of the scamp and how insolently he mocks me? I have a mind to have him and his partner dragged off to prison; for I understand that there are two ringleaders of this gang that has seized practically all the land in the mountains. Yes, and I do not believe they keep their hands off the wrecks that are cast up from time to time, living as they do almost above the rocks off Cape Caphereus.† Where, otherwise, did they get such valuable fields, nay, rather, entire villages,

* The Attic measure or *choinix* was nearly a quart.
† A rocky dangerous promontory at the south-east corner of Euboea.

and such numbers of cattle and draught animals and slaves? Perhaps, too, you note how poor his blouse is and the skin he put on to come here in order to deceive you with the notion that he is evidently a beggar and has nothing. For my part,' said he, 'when I look at him, I am almost frightened, as I fancy I should be if I saw Nauplius * come from Caphereus. I believe he flashes mariners a signal from the heights so as to decoy them on to the rocks.' While he said this and much more besides, the crowd grew ugly, while I was sore perplexed and afraid they might do me some mischief.

"Then another person came forward, a good kindly man, to judge from the words he spoke and from his appearance. He first asked the people to be silent, and they became silent, and then in a quiet tone he said that they who tilled the country's idle land and got it into shape did no wrong, but, on the contrary, deserved commendation. They should not be angry at those who built upon public land and planted trees upon it, but at those who injured it. 'At this moment, sirs,' he said, 'almost two-thirds of our land is a wilderness because of neglect and lack of population. I too own many acres, as I imagine some others do, not only in the mountains but also on the plains, and if anybody would till them, I should not only give him the chance for nothing but gladly pay money besides. For it is plain that they become more valuable to me, and at the same time the sight of land occupied and under cultivation is a pleasing one, while waste lands are not only a useless possession to those who hold them, but very distressing evidence of some mis-

* King of Euboea. In revenge for the death of his son Palamedes at Troy through the treachery of Odysseus, he lighted beacon fires on the promontory as the Greeks were returning and lured many of their ships to destruction.

fortune of their owners. Wherefore, I advise you rather to encourage all the other citizens you can to take some of the public land and work it, those who have some capital taking more, and the poorer citizens as much as each is able to handle, that your land may be in use, and the citizens who accept may be free from two very great evils—idleness and poverty. So let these men have it free for ten years, and after that period let them agree to pay a small portion from their produce but nothing from their cattle. If any alien takes up land, let him likewise pay nothing for the first five years, but after that twice as much as the citizens. And let any alien who shall put fifty acres under cultivation be made a citizen, in order to encourage as many as possible.

" 'At the present moment even the land just outside the city gates is quite wild and terribly unattractive, as though it were in the depths of a wilderness and not in the suburbs of a city, while most of the land inside the walls is sown or grazed. It is therefore surprising that orators trump up charges against the industrious people of Caphereus in the remote parts of Euboea, and yet hold that the men farming the gymnasium and grazing cattle in the market-place are doing nothing out of the way. You can doubtless see for yourselves that they have made your gymnasium into a ploughed field, so that the Heracles and numerous other statues are hidden by the corn, some those of heroes and others those of gods. You see too, day after day, the sheep belonging to this orator invade the market-place at dawn and graze about the council chamber and the executive buildings. Therefore, when strangers first come to our city, they either laugh at it or pity it.' Now on hearing this they burst into a rage against that first speaker in his turn and made a great uproar.

" 'Yet though the accuser does such things, he thinks that humble and needy citizens ought to be haled off to prison, so that no one, forsooth, may do any work hereafter, but that those outside the city may live by brigandage and those within by thievery. I move,' he continued, 'that we leave these men in possession of what they themselves have created, provided they pay a moderate tax hereafter, and that we cancel all arrears to date, since they tilled land that had been wild and valueless and gained possession in that way. If, however, they wish to pay a price for their farm, let us sell to them at a cheaper figure than to anybody else.'

"When he had thus concluded, that first speaker again spoke in reply, and the two stormed at each other for a long time. But finally I was bidden to say whatever I wished.

" 'And what ought I to say?' I asked. 'Reply to what has been said,' cried one from his seat. 'Well then, I declare,' said I, 'that there is not one word of truth in what he has said. And as for me, sirs,' I continued, 'I thought I was dreaming when he prated about fields and villages and such like. We have no village or horses or asses or cattle. I wish we might possess all the good things he described, that we might not only have given to you but might also belong to the wealthy class ourselves! Yet what we even now have is sufficient for us, and do you take whatever you wish of it. Even if you want all, we shall replace it.' At these words they applauded.

"Thereupon the magistrate asked me what we would be able to give to the people, to which I replied, 'Four deer pelts of excellent quality.' Here the majority laughed and the magistrate was vexed at me. 'That is because the bear skins are rough,' I continued, 'and the goat skins are not as good as they. Some are old and some are small. But take these too, if you wish.' Then he was vexed once more and said that I was a downright landloper, and I replied, 'Do I again hear mention of lands, and from you? Did I not tell you that we have no lands?'

"He asked next whether we would agree each to give an Attic talent,* and I replied, 'We do not weigh our meat, but we will give whatever we have. There is a little salted down, but the rest is smoked and not much inferior to the other. There are sides of bacon and venison and other excellent meats.' Then they did raise an uproar and called me a liar. The man also asked me if we had any grain and about how much. I told him the exact amount. 'Three bushels of wheat,' said I, 'six of barley, and the same amount of millet, but only four quarts of beans, since there were none this year. Now do you take the wheat and the barley,' said I, 'and leave us the millet. But if you need millet, take it too.'

" 'And do you not make any wine?' another asked. 'We make it,' I said, 'so that if any one of you comes, we will hand it over, but be sure to bring some kind of wineskin with you, since we haven't any.' 'Now, just how many vines have you?' 'Two,' I replied, 'outside our doors, twenty in the yard, the same number across the river that we set out recently. They are of very fine quality and yield large clusters when the passers-by leave them alone. But to spare you the trouble of asking about every detail, I will tell you what else we have: eight she-goats, a mulley † cow with a very pretty calf, four sickles, four grub hoes, three spears, and each of us owns a hunting knife. As for the

* The speaker referred to the silver money talent worth somewhat more than £200 ($1000). The countryman knew the talent only as a weight, about 85 pounds at that time.
† That is, hornless or polled.

crockery—why should one mention that? We have wives too, and children by them. We live in two pretty huts, and we have a third where the grain and the pelts are kept.'

" 'Yes by heavens,' said the orator, 'where you bury your money too, I suspect.' 'Well then,' said I, 'come and dig it up, you fool! Who buries money in the ground? It certainly does not grow.' Then everybody laughed, and it was at him, I thought.

" 'That is what we have; and now, if you want everything, we are willing to give it to you voluntarily. There is no need for you to take it from us by force as though it belonged to foreigners or rogues; for, mark you, we are citizens too of this city, as I used to hear my father say. And once he too came here just when a grant of money was being made, as it happened, and got some too along with the rest. Therefore we are raising our children to be your fellow-citizens; and should you ever need them, they will help you against brigands and foreign foes. Just now there is peace; but if ever such a crisis does arise, you will pray heaven that the majority be like ourselves. For do not imagine that this talker will fight for you then, unless, indeed, it be to scold like a woman. Besides, whenever we catch any game, we will give you a part of the meat and of the skins; only send someone to get them. Then if you bid us raze our huts, we will do so if they trouble you. But you must give us housing here; else how shall we endure the winter's cold? You have many empty houses inside the city walls; one of them will be enough for us. Yet if we choose to live elsewhere than here and thus avoid adding to the congestion caused by so many people being huddled together, that surely is no reason for moving us.

" 'Then as to that ghoulish and wicked practice in case of wrecked vessels which the speaker had the hardihood to accuse us of—and I almost forgot to speak of it, although I should have done so at the very start—who among you could possibly believe him? Not to mention the impiety of it, it is impossible to salvage anything at all there. Indeed, all the timber you can find there is the splinters, so very small are the fragments cast up. Besides, that is the most inaccessible beach in existence. And the oar-blades which I once found cast ashore—why, I nailed them to the sacred oak that grows by the sea. Pray God I may never get or earn any profit like that from human misfortune! Why, I have never made anything out of it, but many is the time I have pitied shipwrecked travellers who have come to my door, taken them into my hut, given them to eat and to drink, helped them in any other way that I could, and accompanied them until they got out of the wilderness. Yet who of them is there who will testify for me now? And I never did that to win a testimonial or gratitude; why, I never knew where the men came from even. I pray that none of you may ever undergo such an experience.'

"While I was thus speaking, a man rose in their midst, and I thought to myself that perhaps he was another of the same sort who was going to slander me, but he said: 'Sirs, for a long time I have been wondering whether I knew this man, but nevertheless was inclined to think that I did not. But now that I have clearly identified him, it seems to me that it would be dreadful, or rather a crime against heaven, for me not to corroborate his statements as far as I can, or express my gratitude in words after having in very deed received the greatest kindness at his hands. I am,' he continued, 'a citizen here, as you are aware, and so is this man,' pointing to his neighbour, who thereupon rose also. 'Two years ago we happened to be sailing in Socles' boat when it was lost off Caphereus and only a handful of us were saved out of a large number. Now some were sheltered by purple-fishers, for a few had money in their wallets; but we who were cast ashore destitute tramped along a path, hoping to find some shelter among shepherds or herdsmen, for we were in danger of perishing from hunger and thirst. And after much hardship we did finally reach some huts and stopped and hallooed, when this man here came out, brought us in, and made a low fire which he gradually increased. Then he himself rubbed one of us, and his wife the other, with tallow, for they had no olive oil. Finally, they poured warm water over us until they brought us around, chilled to the bone as we had been. Then, after making us recline and throwing about us what they had, they put wheaten loaves before us to eat while they themselves ate millet porridge. They also gave us wine to drink, they themselves drinking water, and they roasted venison in abundance, while some of it they boiled. And though we wanted to go away on the morrow, they held us back for three days. Then they escorted us down to the plains and gave us meat when we left them, as well as a very handsome pelt for each of us. And when this man here saw that I was still ill from my trying experience, he put on me a little tunic which he took from his daughter, and she girded a bit of cloth about herself instead. This I gave back when I reached the village. So, next to the gods, we owe our lives to this man especially.'

"While he was thus speaking, the people listened with pleasure and showed me their approval, and I recalled it all and cried out, 'Hello, Sotades!' And I approached and kissed him and the other man. However, the people laughed heartily because I kissed them. Then I understood that in the cities people do not kiss one another.

"Then that kind and good man who had spoken in my behalf at the beginning came forward and said, 'I move, sirs, that we invite this man to dine in the town-hall. If he had saved one of our townsfolk in battle by covering him with his shield, would he not have received many large gifts? But now, when he has saved two citizens, and perhaps others who are not here, is he entitled to no honour at all? For the tunic which he stripped from his daughter and gave to his fellow-townsman in distress, let the city give him a tunic and a cloak as an inducement to others to be righteous and to help one another. Further, let it vote that they and their children have the use of the farm free from molestation, and that the man himself be given one hundred drachmas for equipment; and as for this money, I offer it out of my own pocket on behalf of the city.'

"For this he was applauded and the motion was carried. The clothes and the money were also brought into the theatre at once. But I was loath to accept, whereupon they said, 'You cannot dine in the skin.' 'Well then,' said I, 'I shall go without dinner to-day.' However, they put the tunic on me and threw the cloak over my shoulders. Then I wanted to throw my skin on top of all, but they would not let me. The money I absolutely refused and swore that I would not take it. 'But if you are hunting for somebody who will take it,' said I, 'give it to that orator that he may bury it, for he knows all about that evidently.' And from that day nobody has bothered us."

Now he had hardly ended when we were at the huts, and laughing I said, "But you have hidden from your fellow-citizens one thing, the fairest of your possessions." "What is that?" said he. "This garden," I replied, "very pretty indeed with all its vegetables and trees." "There was not any then," he said; "we made it afterwards."

Then we entered and feasted the rest of the day, we reclining on boughs and skins that made a high bed and the wife sitting near beside her husband. But a daughter of marriageable age served the food and poured us a sweet dark wine to drink; and the boys prepared the meat, helping themselves as they passed it around, so that I could not help deeming these people fortunate and thinking that of all the men that I knew, they lived the happiest lives. And yet I knew the homes and tables of rich men, of satraps and kings as well as of private individuals; but then they seemed to me the most wretched of all; and though they had so appeared before, yet I felt this the more strongly as I beheld the poverty and free spirit of the humble cottagers and noted that they lacked naught of the joy of eating and drinking, nay, that even in these things they had, one might almost say, the better of it.

We were already well enough supplied when that other man entered, accompanied by his son, a prepossessing lad who carried a hare. The latter on entering commenced to blush; and while his father was welcoming us, he himself kissed the maiden and gave her the hare. The child then ceased serving and sat down beside her mother while the boy served in her stead. "Is she the one," I enquired of my host, "whose tunic you took off and gave to the ship-wrecked man?" "No," said he with a smile, "that daughter was married long ago and already has grown-up children. Her husband is a rich man living in a village." "And do they help you when you need anything?" I enquired. "We do not need anything," replied the wife, "but they get game from us whenever we catch any, and fruit and vege-tables, for they have no garden. Last year we borrowed some wheat just for seed, but we repaid them as soon as harvest time was come." "Tell me," said I, "do you intend to marry this girl also to a rich man that she too may lend you wheat?" At this the two blushed, the girl as well as the boy.

"She will have a poor man for a husband," said the father, "a hunter like ourselves," and with a smile he glanced at the young man. And I said, "But why do you not give her away at once? Must her husband come from some village or other?" "I have an idea," he replied, "that he is not far off; nay, he is here in this house, and we shall celebrate the marriage when we have picked out a good day." "And how do you determine the good day?" said I. And he replied, "When the moon is not in a quarter; the air must be clear too, and the weather fine." And then I said, "Tell me, is he really a good hunter?" "I am," cried the youth; "I can run down a deer and face the charge of a boar. You shall see to-morrow, stranger, if you wish it." "And did you catch this hare?" said I. "Yes," he replied, laughing—"with my net during the night, for the sky was very beautiful, and the moon was never so big before." Then the two men laughed, not only the girl's father but his also. As for him, he felt ashamed and became silent.

Then the girl's father said, "Well, my boy, it is not I who am delaying you, but your father is waiting until he can go and buy a victim, for we must sacrifice to the gods." At this point the girl's younger brother interrupted, saying, "Why, this fellow got a victim long ago. It is being fattened in there behind the hut, and a fine animal it is." "Is it really so?" they asked him, and he said "Yes." "And where did you get it?" they enquired. "When we caught the wild sow that had the young ones, they all escaped but one. They ran more swiftly than the hare," he added. "One, however, I hit with a stone, caught, and covered with my leather jerkin. I exchanged it in the village and got a young pig for it. Then I made a sty out behind and raised it." "So that is the reason why your mother would laugh," exclaimed the father, "when I used to wonder on hearing the pig grunt, and you were using the barley so freely." "Well," he replied, "the chestnuts were not enough to fatten her, supposing she had been willing to eat nuts without anything else. But if you wish to see her, I will go and fetch her in." And they bade him do so. So he and the boys were off at once on the run, full of glee. Meanwhile the girl had risen and brought from another hut some sliced sorb-apples, medlars, winter apples, and swelling clusters of fine grapes, and placed them on the table after wiping off the stains from the meat with leaves and putting some clean fern beneath. Then the boys came in laughing and full of fun, leading the pig, and with them followed the young man's mother and two small brothers. They brought white loaves of wheaten bread, boiled eggs in wooden platters, and parched chickpeas.

After the woman had greeted her brother and her niece, his daughter, she sat down beside her husband and said, "See, there is the victim which that boy has long been feeding for his wedding day, and everything else is ready on our side. The barley and wheaten flour have been ground; only perhaps we shall need a little more wine. This too we can easily get from the village." And close beside her stood her son, glancing at his future father-in-law. He smiled at the lad and said, "There is the one who is holding things up. I believe he wants to fatten the pig a bit more." The young man replied, "Why, she is ready to burst with fat." And wishing to help him, I said, "Take care that your young man doesn't get thin while the pig gets fat." "Our guest speaks well," said the mother, "for he has already grown thinner than I have ever seen him before; and I noticed a short time ago that he was wakeful in the night and went out of the hut." "The dogs were barking," the young man interrupted, "and I went out to see." "No, you did not," said she, "but you were walking around distraught. So don't let us permit him to be tortured any longer." And throwing her arms about the girl's mother she kissed her; and the latter, turning to her husband, said, "Let us do as they wish." This they decided to do and said, "Let us have the wedding the day after to-morrow." They also invited me to stay over, and I did so gladly, at the same time reflecting on the character of weddings and other things among the rich, on the matchmakers, the scrutinies of property and birth, the dowries, the gifts from the bridegroom, the promises and deceptions, the contracts and agreements, and, finally, the wranglings and enmities that often occur at the wedding itself.

Now I have not told this long story idly or, as some might perhaps infer, with the desire to spin a yarn, but to present an illustration of the manner of life that I adopted at the beginning and of the life of the poor—an illustration drawn from my own experience for anyone who wishes to consider whether in words and deeds and in social intercourse the poor are at a disadvantage in comparison with the rich on account of their poverty, so far as living a seemly and natural life is concerned, or in every way have the advantage. And really, when I consider Euripides' words and ask myself whether as a matter of fact the entertainment of strangers is so difficult for them that they can never welcome or succour anyone in need, I find this by no means to be true of their hospitality. They light a fire more promptly than the rich and guide one on the way without reluctance—indeed, in such matters a sense of self-respect would compel them—and often they share what they have more readily. When will you find a rich man who will give the victim of a shipwreck his wife's or his daughter's purple gown or any article of clothing far cheaper than that: a mantle, for example, or a tunic, though he has thousands of them, or even a cloak from one of his slaves?

CHAEREAS AND CALLIRHOE
BY CHARITON

The adventure-story of Chaereas and Callirhoe, of which the first chapter, out of eight, is given here, is the first surviving European novel, the predecessor of a million others. Some scraps of the text recently discovered in Egypt help to date it about A.D. 150, or perhaps earlier. Primitive as the novel is, it manifests considerable narrative skill. Of the author, Chariton, we know no more than he tells us in his opening sentence, that he was a clerk or secretary to a lawyer in Aphrodisias, near the present Izmir in Asia Minor. The site of Aphrodisias is now being actively excavated; perhaps our author will be exhumed along with artifacts and inscriptions.

The translation of Chariton's *Chaereas and Callirhoe* by Warren E. Blake, who also edited and published the Greek text, was published by the University of Michigan Press (Ann Arbor) in 1939; copyright 1939 by the University of Michigan. The selection is used by permission of the publisher.

I AM CHARITON OF APHRODISIA, secretary to the advocate Athenagoras, and I am going to tell you about a love affair that took place in Syracuse. Hermocrates, general of Syracuse, the one who defeated the Athenians,* had a daughter named Callirhoe, a wonderful sort of girl and the admiration of all Sicily. Really her loveliness was hardly human; it was divine,—and it was not that of a mere nymph of the sea or the mountains, either, but of Aphrodite the Maiden. The fame of this incredible vision of beauty spread far and wide and suitors came pouring into Syracuse, potentates and royal princes, not only from Sicily, but from Italy, Epirus, and the nations of the Asiatic

* In 414 B.C. The story is thus set at the time of the Pelopponesian War.—Ed.

continent. But the god of love wanted to make a match of his own devising.

Now there was a certain young man called Chaereas, better looking than all the rest, who resembled the statues and pictures of Achilles and Nireus and Hippolytus and Alcibiades. His father was Ariston, second in rank only to Hermocrates in Syracuse. There was a political rivalry between the two, which would have led either of them to make an alliance with any family sooner than with that of the other. However, Love thrives on opposition and delights in accomplishing unexpected results, and this was the opportunity for which he was looking.

There was a public festival of Aphrodite and almost all the women had gone off to her temple. Callirhoe until now had never appeared in public, but at her father's command her mother brought her out to worship the goddess. Just then Chaereas was walking home from the gymnasium, radiant as a star. The flush of exercise bloomed on his glowing face like gold on silver. Now as it happened, these two came upon each other at a narrow corner face to face, —a meeting shrewdly contrived by the god to insure their seeing each other. Immediately they fell in love, since beauty had met with nobility.

Like a hero mortally wounded in battle, ashamed to fall, but unable to stand, Chaereas could barely go off home with his wound. As for the girl, she fell at the feet of Aphrodite, kissed them, and said, "Lady, give me as my husband this man whom thou hast shown me!"

Night came on, dreadful to both, for love's fire was kindled. Yet the girl's suffering was more severe because she had to keep silent in shame of being discovered. But when Chaereas began to waste away, being a young man of good disposition and proud spirit, he had the courage to tell his parents that he was in love and could not live unless he won Callirhoe as his wife. On hearing this, his father groaned and said, "My boy, your case is hopeless. Hermocrates, I am sure, would never give you his daughter when she has so many other suitors of wealth and royal rank. No, you must not even attempt it, or we may be openly insulted."

His father then tried to comfort the boy, but his trouble grew, so that he no longer appeared in public to engage in his usual pursuits. The gymnasium felt the loss of Chaereas and was practically deserted, for the young people loved him. By persistent inquiry they learned the cause of his illness, and they all felt sincere pity for this handsome young man who was in danger of death from the honest passion of his heart.

A formal public assembly was called. When the people had taken their seats, their first and only demand was this, "Noble Hermocrates, mighty general, save Chaereas! Let this be the greatest of your triumphs. Our city intercedes for the marriage today of these two who are so worthy of each other."

Who could describe that assembly of which the god of love was the spokesman? Hermocrates, as a true patriot, was unable to refuse the demands of the state. So when he nodded his assent, all the people leaped to their feet and ran from the theater. The young men went off after Chaereas while the senators and officials followed along with Hermocrates. Even the women of Syracuse were there to conduct the bride to her home. The marriage hymn was chanted throughout all the city, the narrow lanes were filled with garlands and torches, and the vestibules were sprinkled with wine and perfumes. The Syracusans celebrated this day with greater delight than the day of their victory.

Now the girl knew nothing of this and had thrown

herself with covered head upon her couch, silently weeping. Her nurse came to her bed and said, "Get up, my child. The day has come which we all have wanted most. The city is celebrating your wedding."

"Her knees and heart were unstrung," as Homer says, for she did not know to whom she was being married. Immediately she became speechless, and a blackness spread over her eyes and she nearly fainted. To those that saw her, this appeared to be her modesty. But as soon as her maids had dressed her, the crowd at her doors went away, and the parents of the bridegroom brought him to the girl. And so Chaereas ran forward and kissed her, and Callirhoe, recognizing her lover, became more stately and lovely than ever, as a flickering lamp again flares up when oil is poured in.

When she went out to appear in public, astonishment overcame all the crowd just as when Artemis appears to hunters in lonely places. Indeed, many of those present even fell down to worship her. All admired Callirhoe and congratulated Chaereas. The wedding was much like that of Thetis, which, as the poets sing, took place in Pelion. Yet here, too, was found a demon of envy just as there, they say, was the goddess of strife.

The suitors who had failed to win the bride felt both grief and anger. Though hitherto they had quarreled with each other, they now came to an understanding, and through this understanding and a sense of the insult they had received, they joined in common counsel, and envy was their leader in their attack upon Chaereas.

First a young man from Italy, the prince of Rhegium, stood up and spoke as follows: "If any one of us had married her, I should not have been angry, for, just as in the athletic games, one man only among the contestants must be the victor; but since he has surpassed us without working to win his bride, I cannot bear the insult. As for us, we have wasted away, keeping sleepless nights before the door of her house, flattering nurses and maids, and sending gifts to her attendants. How long we have been slaves! And what is worst of all, we have come to hate each other as rivals. But this dirty rascal, poverty-stricken and the lowest of the low, in a contest with kings has borne off the crown for himself without a struggle. Let us see to it that he does not enjoy his prize, and let us turn the wedding into death for the groom."

They all applauded, and only the ruler of Agrigentum objected. "It is not," he said, "through any good will toward Chaereas that I am holding up your plans against him, but through considerations of greater safety. Remember that Hermocrates is not a man lightly to be despised, so that it is impossible for us to attack him openly. A crafty approach is better, for it is by unscrupulous deceit rather than brute force that we obtain power. Elect me general of this campaign against Chaereas and I promise you I will dissolve the marriage. I shall arm Jealousy against him, and she, with Love as her ally, can accomplish serious damage. Callirhoe may be even-tempered and incapable of low-minded suspicions, but Chaereas, trained as he is in the gymnasia and not inexperienced in youthful follies, can easily be made suspicious and thus fall into youthful jealousy. Also it is easier to approach him and speak with him."

While he was still talking, they all voted approval of his plan and intrusted the execution of it to him as a man of infinite resource. This then was the scheme on which he set to work.

It was evening, and a messenger came reporting that Ariston, Chaereas' father, had fallen from a ladder on his farm and that there was very little hope of his surviving. Though Chaereas was very fond of his father, he was even more distressed when he heard this, because he had to go alone, since it was not as yet proper to take his bride out with him.

During that night, while no one dared to visit his house in open revelry, yet men did come secretly and unobserved and quietly left behind them the evidence of a wild celebration. They hung wreaths upon the vestibule and sprinkled it with perfumes; they soaked the ground with wine and tossed half-burned torches about.

Day dawned and every passer-by stopped with the universal instinct of curiosity. Now that his father was feeling more comfortable, Chaereas was hurrying back to his wife. Seeing the crowd before the door, he was at first astonished, but when he learned the cause, he rushed in as though possessed. Finding the chamber still shut, he knocked vigorously. But when the maid had opened the door and he had stumbled in to Callirhoe's presence, his anger was changed to sorrow and he tore his clothes and shed tears. When she asked him what had happened, he was speechless, being able neither to disbelieve what he had seen, nor yet to believe what was so contrary to his wishes.

As he stood confused and trembling, his wife, quite unsuspicious of what had happened, begged him to tell her the reason for his anger. With bloodshot eyes and thick voice he said, "It is the fact that you have so quickly forgotten me that hurts so much," and he reproached her for the celebration.

But she, being the daughter of a general and full of pride, grew angry at the unjustice of the accusation and said, "There has been no celebration to disgrace my father's house. Perhaps your vestibule may be used to such things, and your dear friends may be resenting your marriage."

Saying this she turned away and covered her head, and the tears welled forth. Yet reconciliation between lovers is easy and they gladly accept any apology from each other. Thus Chaereas, changing his tone, began to coax and flatter her, and his wife quickly accepted his repentance with joy. This increased the ardor of their love all the more, and the parents of both congratulated themselves when they saw the oneness of mind of their children.

When his first device had fallen through, the suitor from Agrigentum then engaged upon another more effective one, and this was the nature of his contrivance. He had a dependent who was ready of speech and full of every social grace. He gave orders to him to act the part of a lover, since he was trying to make a friendly accomplice of Callirhoe's favorite maid whom she most highly valued of all her servants. After some difficulty this person succeeded in winning the girl over with generous gifts, and declaring that unless he gained her love he would hang himself. A woman is easily taken in when she thinks that she is loved.

After making these preparations, the director of this drama discovered another actor, not equally attractive, but a clever rascal and a persuasive talker. When he had given him preliminary instructions as to what he must do and say, he sent him secretly to Chaereas as a stranger.

Coming up to him as he was wandering about near the wrestling grounds, he said, "Chaereas, I too had a son of just your age who greatly admired and loved you when he was alive. Now that he is dead, I consider you as my son,—indeed, you and your happiness are a common blessing to all Sicily. Give me a little of your time and you shall hear of important matters which concern your whole life."

With these words this abominable rogue set the young man's heart aflutter and filled him with hope, fear, and curiosity. But when he begged him to speak, the other hesitated and pretended that the present occasion was not suitable and that they needed further delay and a longer time. Chaereas insisted all the more, expecting by now something rather serious.

The other took him by the right hand and led him off to a quiet spot. Then, contracting his brows, and assuming an expression of sorrow, and shedding a few tears besides, he said, "Chaereas, it is not pleasant for me to tell you of this sad business, and though I long have wanted to speak, I have hesitated. But now that you are being openly disgraced and the horrible thing is being discussed everywhere, I can no longer stand it to keep quiet. I am a man who naturally hates wrong, and I feel especially kindly toward you. You must know then that your wife is a partner in adultery and, to prove this to you, I am ready to show you the adulterer in the very act."

"Thus spake he, and a black cloud of grief enwrapped him, and with both hands he took dark dust and poured it over his head and defiled his comely face." * For a long time Chaereas remained in a daze, unable to speak or raise his eyes. When he had recovered, he said in a voice that was unnatural and weak, "It is a miserable favor indeed to ask of you, to make me an eye-witness of my own troubles. Yet show him to me so that I may have greater reason for killing myself, for even though Callirhoe is guilty too, I shall spare her."

"Pretend," said the other, "that you are going away to the country. Then late in the evening keep watch on the house and you shall see her lover go in."

* A quotation from Homer.—Ed.

So they agreed, and Chaereas sent in a messenger, since he could not endure even to go in there himself, and said, "I am going away to the country." Then the black-hearted villain set the scene of his drama.

When evening came, Chaereas took his place of observation while the other man, who had corrupted Callirhoe's maid, darted up the narrow lane, acting as though he preferred to get at his business in secret, but actually managing it all so as not to be overlooked. He had long lustrous hair with locks scented with perfume; his eyes were lined with cosmetics; his cloak was soft; his shoes were light and fine; heavy rings gleamed on his fingers. Next, looking carefully around, he approached the door and knocking lightly, gave the usual sign. The maid, also in great trepidation, softly opened the door and taking him by the hand, led him in. Seeing this, Chaereas could no longer restrain himself but rushed in to seize the adulterer on the spot. He, however, had taken his stand beside the door of the courtyard and quickly ran out.

Callirhoe was sitting on her couch longing for Chaereas and had not even lighted a lamp because of her sorrow. There came the sound of footsteps and she was first aware of her husband by his heavy breathing, and ran with joy to greet him. But he had no voice with which to reproach her; instead, overwhelmed with anger, he kicked at his wife as she ran forward, and his foot struck her squarely in the middle and stopped short her breath. She fell on the floor and her maidservants picked her up and laid her upon the bed. And so Callirhoe lay without speech or breath, presenting to all the appearance of death.

Rumor ran throughout the city reporting what had happened, and aroused cries of grief throughout the narrow streets down to the sea. From every side lamentations resounded, and the affair was very like the capture of a city. Chaereas, still inwardly seething, locked himself in a room and throughout the night severely examined the maidservants, first and last Callirhoe's favorite, and he learned the truth in the course of torturing them with fire and whips. Then his heart was overcome with pity for his dead wife and he longed to kill himself, but was prevented by Polycharmus, a particular friend of his, just as Patroclus was to Achilles in Homer.

When day came, the officials empaneled a jury for the murder trial, hurrying the case out of respect for Hermocrates. The whole populace, too, rapidly assembled in the market place, with various shouts and exclamations. The unsuccessful suitors sought the favor of the crowd, and especially the man from Agrigentum, with the imposing and dignified manner of one who has accomplished some utterly unexpected result.

A strange thing now took place, the like of which had never before occurred in a courtroom. After the charge had been made, the murderer, instead of defending himself when his time had been allotted him by the water clock, brought still more bitter accusations against himself and was the first to cast the vote of condemnation. He said nothing that was appropriate to his defense, not mentioning the slanderous attack, nor his jealousy, nor his lack of premeditation, but begged them all, "Stone me to death in public. I have robbed our people of their crown. It is an act of mercy if you hand me over to the executioner. This ought to be my fate if it were only a maidservant of Hermocrates whom I had killed. Look for some unspeakable kind of punishment. I have committed a crime worse than temple-robbing or parricide. Do not bury me. Do not pollute the earth but sink my sinful body in the depths of the sea!"

At these words a cry of grief broke forth and every one deserted the cause of the dead woman and mourned for the living man.

Hermocrates was the first to counsel Chaereas. "I know," he said, "that what happened was unintended. I have my eyes on the conspirators. They shall not enjoy the sight of two corpses, and I shall not offend the memory of my daughter. Indeed I have heard her say many times that she had rather Chaereas should live than herself. Let us put a stop to this useless court trial and go out to the tomb that none may escape. Let us not give up her body to the ravages of time nor allow it to lose its beauty through decay. Let us bury Callirhoe while she is still beautiful."

Accordingly the jury cast the vote of acquittal. Chaereas, however, would not acquit himself but longed for death and was arranging every means of accomplishing his end. Polycharmus, seeing that it was impossible to save him in any other way, said, "Traitor to the dead, will you not wait even to bury Callirhoe? Will you trust her body to the hands of others? Now is the time for you to provide rich funeral offerings and to prepare a royal funeral procession." This speech was persuasive, for it inspired in him feelings of pride and responsibility.

Who could worthily describe that funeral procession? Callirhoe, clothed in her bridal garments, lay upon a golden bier, more stately and beautiful than ever, so that they all compared her to the sleeping Ariadne. Ahead of the bier came first the knights of Syracuse, themselves and their horses in full regalia; after them were heavy-armed soldiers carrying the standards of Hermocrates' triumphs; then the senate; and in the center, the assembly, all acting as bodyguards to Hermocrates. Ariston, too, was carried along, since he was still weak, and he called Callirhoe his daughter and mistress. After these were the women of the citizens clad in black; next, a royal wealth of funeral offerings, first the gold and silver of the dowry, a beautiful array of clothing (for Hermocrates had contributed much from the spoils of war), and the gifts of relatives and friends. Last of all followed the rich possessions of Chaereas, since it was his wish, if possible, to burn all his property at the burial of his wife. The young men of Syracuse carried the bier and the rabble followed behind. Amid the lamentations of all, the voice of Chaereas was distinctly heard.

There was a magnificent tomb belonging to Hermocrates near the shore, so as to be visible even to people far out at sea. This was filled like a treasure-house with the abundant richness of the funeral gifts. However, what was intended to serve as a mark of respect to the dead, brought about the beginning of still greater happenings.

There was a rascal called Theron who followed a criminal career upon the sea. He was in command of freebooters who secretly rode at anchor in the harbors, pretending to be ferry-men, and thus he organized his business of piracy. He had happened to be present at the funeral procession and had fixed his eyes on the gold, and at night when he lay down to sleep he could not rest.

"Am I to risk my life," he said to himself, "battling with the sea and committing murders for a mere pittance when there is a chance to get rich from one lone corpse? No! It is settled. I will not pass by this profit. But whom shall I enlist for this business? Think carefully, Theron. Who of those you know is fit for the job? Zenophanes, of Thurium? He is shrewd, but he is a coward. Menon of Messenia? He is daring enough, but a traitor." Going over each man in his thoughts, and as it were, testing their metal, he rejected most of them, but considered a few as suitable.

At early dawn he ran down to the harbor and looked up each of them. Some he found in the brothels and some in the taverns, a gang well worthy of such a leader. Saying that he had something of great importance to tell them, he led them off back of the harbor and began with these words: "I have found a treasure, and I have chosen you of all men to share it with me. There is no mere one-man profit in this, and yet there is not much effort required either, but a single night's work can make us all rich. We are no strangers to business of this sort, which fools may condemn, but sensible men may turn to advantage."

They understood at once that he was proposing some piece of piracy or tomb-breaking or temple-robbing and said, "Stop trying to persuade us when we are already persuaded. Just tell us what the business is, and let us not lose our time."

"You have seen the gold and silver with the corpse," said Theron in reply. "This should more rightly belong to us, the living. I propose to open up the tomb at night and then to load our boat and sail away wherever the wind may take us and sell our cargo in a foreign land."

They were delighted.

"Now," said he, "go back again to your usual occupations. Late in the evening each one of you come down to the boat bringing a builder's tool."

This they did, and Callirhoe and her fortunes met with a new and more dreadful sort of resurrection. When lack of food had produced in her some degree of recovery from her suspended animation, she slowly and gradually regained her breath. Then she began to stir, one limb after another, and opening her eyes she regained consciousness as though waking from sleep, and called Chaereas, thinking he was sleeping beside her. But when neither her husband nor her servants heard her, and everything remained deserted and dark, a shudder of horror came over the poor girl, unable as she was by any exercise of reason to guess the truth.

Scarcely had she awakened, when her hands touched the funeral wreaths and ribbons. Her movements created a rattling of gold and silver. There was a prevalent odor of spices. Then, at last, she recalled the blow she had received and the fall that resulted from it, and reluctantly and with anguish she recognized the tomb.

Thereupon she broke the silence with a shout, as loud as she could utter, crying, "I am alive! Save me!"

But when she had cried many times and nothing further occurred, she gave up all hope of rescue, and bending her head on her knees she lamented.

"Oh, dreadful fate!" she said. "I have been buried alive though I did no wrong, and I am to die a lingering death. They mourn me as dead, though I am well. Whom can I find to send them a message? Cruel Chaereas, I blame you, not for causing my death, but because you were so hasty in casting me out from the house. You should not have buried Callirhoe so soon, not even if she were really dead. But perhaps you already have plans for remarriage!"

While she was thus engaged in incoherent lamentation, Theron, waiting until midnight, was noiselessly approaching the tomb, stroking the water lightly with his oars. Stepping ashore first, he assigned the duties of his crew in this way. He dispatched four men to keep watch in case anyone should approach the place, to kill them if they could, otherwise to give notice of their arrival by signal. He and four others proceeded to the tomb. As for the rest (there were eleven altogether) he told them to wait on board the boat and to keep the oars poised so that if any emergency arose, they could quickly pick up those on shore and sail away.

When the crowbars were applied, and the pounding grew louder as they broke into the tomb, Callirhoe was seized all at once with fear, joy, grief, amazement, hope, and disbelief.

"What does this noise mean? Has some divinity come to seek me in my misery, as is common in the experience of the dying? Or is this not mere noise, but the voice of the gods below who are calling me to them? It is more likely that they are tomb-robbers. So this, too, has been added to my misfortunes! Wealth is useless to a corpse."

While she was still seeking some explanation, the robber bent his head and entered the tomb a little way. Callirhoe fell down before him in her desire to beg mercy, but he leaped back in terror and with a trembling voice shouted to his comrades, "Let us get out of here. Some ghost is on guard in there and will not let us come in."

Theron laughed him to scorn, calling him a coward and more of a corpse than the dead woman herself. Then he ordered another man to go in, and when no one dared to do so, he entered himself, holding out his sword before him.

At the gleam of the steel, Callirhoe shrank back into the extreme corner of the tomb in fear of death, and from there she begged him in a small voice, "Whoever you are, have mercy on me, for I have obtained no mercy from either husband or parents. Do not kill me now that you have rescued me."

Theron gained more courage and, being a shrewd man, realized the truth. He stood there in deep thought and at first planned to kill the girl, thinking she would prove a hindrance to the whole undertaking. But with an eye to possible profit, he quickly changed his mind and said to himself, "She too can be a part of the funeral treasure. There is plenty of silver and gold here, but the beauty of the girl is more valuable than all of this."

So taking her by the hand he led her out. Then calling his assistant he said, "Look, here is the ghost that scared you. A fine buccaneer you are, to be afraid of a woman! Keep watch of her now, for I intend to give her back to her parents. As for us, let us bring out the stuff that is stored inside, now that no longer even the corpse is guarding it."

When they had filled the boat with the loot, Theron ordered the guard to stand a little to one side with the girl. Then he put before them the question as to what to do with her.

Various and contradictory opinions were expressed and the first speaker said, "Comrades, we came for one thing and, as fortune would have it, it has turned out to be something better. Let us take advantage of it. We can get the business done without risk. I propose to leave the tomb treasure right here and to give Callirhoe back to her husband and father and say that we anchored near the place in the course of our regular fishing and that on hearing a cry we opened the tomb out of pity so as to rescue her from her imprisonment. Let us make the girl swear to give full support to our testimony. She will be glad to do so out of gratitude to the kind friends who saved her. Just think with what joy we shall fill all Sicily, and the big rewards we shall get! At the same time we shall be doing the honest thing in the sight of men and the pious thing in the sight of heaven."

But before he had finished, another objected. "Misguided fool," he said, "are you telling us to play the philosopher at this stage? Has robbing a tomb made decent people of us? Shall we show her mercy when her own husband refused to do so and killed her? She has done us no harm, you say. But she will do us the greatest possible harm. In the first place, if we give her back to her relatives, there is no telling what attitude they will take about the matter, and it is impossible for them not to suspect the reason for our coming to the tomb. Also, even if the girl's relatives do forego any punishment of us, still the public officials and the people themselves will not let off tomb-robbers who are convicted by the very wares they bring. The life we lead is not without danger in any case. Perhaps someone may say that it is more profitable to sell the girl, since she will fetch a high price because of her beauty. But this, too, has its dangers. Gold has no voice and silver will not tell where we got it. About them we can make up any story we want. But who can hide away property which has eyes, ears, and a tongue? And besides, hers is no mere human beauty to help us avoid detection. Shall we say that she is a slave? Who will believe that, once he sees her? Therefore, let us kill her right here and let us not carry around a living accusation against ourselves." Though many agreed with these words, Theron put neither proposition to the vote.

"Your proposal," he said, "is dangerous. You, on the other hand, are ruining our profit. I will sell the girl rather than kill her. While she is on sale she will keep quiet through fear, and once sold let her bring her charges, when we are no longer there. Get on board. Let us sail. It is already near dawn."

The ship, when it put to sea, rode splendidly, for they

did not force their way against wind and waves, having no special course laid out before them. Every wind seemed favorable to them and stood at the stern.

Theron sought to comfort Callirhoe, trying to deceive her with all kinds of notions. But she was aware of her situation, and knew that she had been rescued in vain. She pretended, however, not to know this, but to believe him, in fear that after all he might kill her if she seemed resentful. So, saying that she could not endure the sea, she covered her head and wept.

"In this very sea, father," she said, "you once defeated three hundred warships of the Athenians, and now one small vessel is bearing off your daughter and you cannot help me. I am being carried away to a strange land and I, a girl of noble birth, must be a slave. Perhaps some Athenian master will buy the daughter of Hermocrates! How much better it would be for me to lie dead in the tomb! Then, at any rate, Chaereas would have been buried with me. But now we have been parted both in life and in death."

Such were her lamentations. Meantime the robbers sailed past the smaller islands and towns, since their cargo was not suited for poor men, but they were looking for persons of wealth. Presently they anchored down by a mole opposite the coast of Attica, where there was a spring of pure, abundant water and a pleasant meadow. Taking Callirhoe there from out the boat, they required her to refresh herself and to get a little rest from the sea, wishing to preserve her beauty.

When they were alone, they proceeded to consider what course they should now set, and one man said, "Athens is nearby, a great and prosperous city. There we shall find a great number of dealers and an abundance of wealthy men.

You can see as many whole cities in Athens as there are men in a market place."

So they all thought it best to sail down to Athens.

But Theron did not care for the peculiar officiousness of that town. "Is it possible," he said, "that you have not heard of the meddlesome curiosity of the Athenians? They are a talkative people and fond of lawsuits, and in the harbor shysters without number will try to find out who we are and where we got this cargo. Vile suspicions will fill their evil minds. The Areopagus is near at hand and their officials are sterner than tyrants. We may well fear the Athenians more than the Syracusans. The proper place for us is Ionia, where, as you know, there is royal wealth which comes flowing in from mighty Asia, and the people there enjoy luxury and are easy-going. Also I expect to find some acquaintances of mine there."

So after drawing a supply of water and taking on provisions from some nearby freighters, they sailed straight for Miletus and on the third day they arrived at an anchorage most suitable to receive them, about ten miles distant from the city.

Theron then gave orders to take out the oars from the boat and to construct a shelter for Callirhoe and to provide everything for her comfort. This he did not so much from compassion as from love of gain, and more as a trader than a pirate.

He himself hastened down to the town, taking with him two of his companions. Then, having no intention of seeking a purchaser openly nor of making his business the town talk, he tried to hurry through a private sale with no bargaining. But it proved hard to manage, inasmuch as the property was not suited for many people nor for the ordinary man at all, but rather for some wealthy and royal patron, and he was afraid to approach men of this sort.

Consequently, after considerable time had been wasted, he no longer dared to put up with the delay, but when night came, he was unable to sleep, and said to himself, "Theron, you are a fool. You have left behind your gold and silver for all these days in a deserted place as though you were the only pirate in existence. Don't you know that other pirates, also, sail the sea? Then, too, I am afraid that our own men may desert us and sail away. Remember, you did not enlist the most honest men in the world, who would keep faith with you, but rather the biggest rascals you knew. Well," he said, "go to sleep now if you must, but when day comes, hurry down to the boat and throw overboard that misplaced nuisance of a woman, and don't take on any more cargoes so hard to dispose of."

Falling asleep, he dreamed of seeing locked doors, and so he determined to hold on for that day. In the course of his wanderings, he took a seat in a certain workshop, his spirits in utter confusion. Meantime a crowd of men, both free and slave, was passing by, and in the midst of them a man of mature age, clothed in black and sad of face.

Theron rose to his feet (for man is by nature curious) and inquired of one of the attendants, "Who is this man?"

The other replied, "I think you must be a stranger or come from a long way off if you do not recognize Dionysius, a man who is far above all the rest of the Ionians in wealth, ancestry, and education, and a friend of the Great King besides."

"Then why is he wearing black?"

"His dearly beloved wife has died."

Theron sought to prolong the conversation further, now that he had found a man who was rich and romantically inclined, and so he refused to let him go, and inquired, "What position do you hold with him?"

"I am the manager of his whole estate," he replied, "and I am taking care of his daughter, too, a mere baby, left an untimely orphan by the death of her mother."

"And what is your name?"

"Leonas."

"How lucky that I met you, Leonas," he said. "I am a trader just now sailing in from Italy, and that is why I know nothing of affairs in Ionia. A lady of Sybaris, the wealthiest in the city, had a very beautiful maid whom she put up for sale, because she was jealous of her, and I bought her. You can profit by this, if you want to get yourself a nurse for the child (she is well enough trained for that), or if you should consider it worth while to win the good will of your master. You see, it is more to your advantage for him to have a slave he has bought than for him to bring in a stepmother for the girl over your head."

Leonas was delighted to hear this and said, "Heaven must have sent you to be my benefactor. You are displaying to me in daylight the very things I've dreamed of. Come to my house now and be my friend and guest. I can decide about taking this woman when I see whether she is a possession worthy of my master or is merely in our class."

When they came to the house, Theron was astonished at its size and magnificence, for it had been prepared to receive the Great King of Persia. Leonas told him to wait while he first attended to the needs of his master. Then he took him and brought him up to his own room, which was very much like that of a free man, and gave orders to set the table. Theron, a shrewd person and clever in adapting himself to every occasion, helped himself to the food and made himself agreeable to Leonas by frequently drinking to his health. This was partly to demonstrate his frank good nature, but still more to inspire confidence in their partnership. Meantime there was considerable conversation about the girl, and Theron kept praising her good character rather than her beauty, knowing that invisible qualities require an advocate, whereas appearance recommends itself.

"Let us go, then," said Leonas. "Show her to me."

"She is not here," he replied. "We avoided coming to the city because of the customs officials and our boat is anchored about ten miles away,"—and he described the place.

"You are anchored on our own estate," said Leonas, "and that is so much the better. Fortune is plainly bringing you to Dionysius. So let us go down to the farm, and you can recover from your voyage. Our country house nearby is luxuriously furnished."

Theron was still more delighted, thinking that the transaction would be easier in a lonely place than in the open market.

"Let us start out at dawn," he said, "you to the country house, and I to my ship, and I will bring the girl from there to you."

So they agreed and after shaking hands they parted. The night seemed long to both, since one was eager to buy and the other to sell.

On the following day Leonas sailed down the coast to the country house, at the same time bringing with him some money to establish his prior claim with the dealer. Theron meanwhile arrived at the beach and was warmly welcomed by his confederates. After telling them what he had done, he began to coax Callirhoe.

"My daughter," said he, "at first I wanted to take you back to your people, but when a contrary wind came up, I was completely prevented by the condition of the sea. I want you to realize what great care I have taken of you. Most important of all, I have preserved your honor. Chaereas shall get you back unharmed and saved by us, as it were, from the chamber of the tomb. Now we must continue our course to Lycia, but there is no need for you to undergo pointless hardships, especially when you suffer so from seasickness. And so I am going to entrust you to faithful friends here and when I come back I will pick you up and take great pains to bring you back once more to Syracuse. Take any of your things you want. We will keep the rest for you also."

At this Callirhoe smiled to herself, greatly troubled though she was, for she realized his utter absurdity. She knew that she was being sold, but in her desire to be rid of the pirates she regarded this sale as a greater good fortune than her former freedom.

"Father," she said, "I thank you for your kind consideration toward me. May Heaven grant to all of you the reward you deserve. But I think it is unlucky to make use of the funeral offerings. Take good care of them all for me. That little ring which I wore as a corpse is enough for me."

Then covering her head she said, "Theron, take me wherever you want. Any place is better than the sea and the tomb."

When he got near to the country house, Theron arranged the following device. Uncovering Callirhoe's head and loosening her hair, he opened the door and told her to go in first. Leonas and all in the room were struck with amazement at her sudden appearance and some of them thought they had seen a goddess. There was, you see, a story that in the fields Aphrodite showed herself to mortals.

In the midst of their astonishment, Theron, who followed after her, approached Leonas and said, "Stand up and get ready to take the girl. She is the one you want to buy."

Joy and amazement on the part of all followed upon his words. Sending Callirhoe off to bed in the finest room in the house, they allowed her to rest, since she was badly in need of recovering from her grief, weariness, and anxiety.

Theron then took Leonas by the hand and said, "My part of the bargain has been faithfully carried out. You may take the girl right now—after all you are a friend of mine—and go to the city and get your title to her registered, and then you can pay me any price you want."

But Leonas, wishing to return the compliment, said, "Not at all. I will trust you with the money now before registering the title,"—and he wanted to establish his prior claim at once, in fear that the other would change his mind, because he knew there would be many eager purchasers in the city.

So he produced a thousand pieces of silver and tried to make Theron take them. Theron, with an affectation of indifference, accepted them. But when Leonas tried to detain him for dinner (the hour being now late) he said, "I want to sail up to the city this evening, but we will meet each other tomorrow at the harbor."

With this agreement they parted, and Theron went to his ship and gave orders to hoist the anchors and to put out to sea as quickly as possible before they were found out.

Thus while they made their escape, borne along by the breeze, Callirhoe, now left alone, was free to bewail her fate.

"Behold," she said, "yet another tomb more lonely than the first, in which Theron has enclosed me! There my father and mother might have come to see me and Chaereas might have poured forth his tribute of tears. Even in death, I should have thrilled to that. But what friend have I here to call on? Cruel Fortune, hast thou not yet had thy fill of my troubles throughout land and sea? First thou didst make my lover to be my murderer. Chaereas, who never had struck even a slave, launched a mortal blow at me, who loved him. Then thou didst surrender me to the hands of tomb-robbers and didst bring me forth from the tomb to the sea and didst set over me sea-robbers more awful than the very waves. It was for this that I was given the beauty which men acclaim, that Theron, a pirate, might win a great price for me! I have been sold in a lonely place and was not even brought to the city as any other slave might be, for it was thy fear, O Fortune, that if any saw me, they might judge me noble born. That is why I have been handed over like a mere chattel to I know not whom, whether Greeks or barbarians or pirates once again."

As she beat her breast with her hand, she saw on her ring the image of Chaereas, and kissing it, she said, "Chaereas, now truly I am lost to you, parted from you by this mighty deep. You are repenting in grief as you sit by the empty tomb, bearing witness after my death to my innocence, while I, the daughter of Hermocrates, your wife, today have been sold to a master!"

As she thus lamented, sleep gradually came upon her.

[Callirhoe, despairing, is persuaded to marry her master, the governor of Miletus. Chaereas searches for Callirhoe; he is taken prisoner and sold as a slave. The scene changes to Babylon, where King Artaxerxes falls in love with Callirhoe. Chaereas gains his freedom and leads an Egyptian army against Artaxerxes. He finds Callirhoe among his captives and triumphantly returns with her to Syracuse.]

TRUE HISTORY
BY LUCIAN

Lucian, of Samosata on the Euphrates, in northern Syria, lived from about A.D. 115 to 200. He traveled far, as far as France, and ended in Egypt, in some sort of public office, probably a sinecure. He wrote abundantly; some eighty works remain. He was a wit and a mocker, a born debunker, in a disillusioned era congenial to debunking.

His *True History* is a satire on the tall tales and preposterous adventure-stories of the Greek classics, especially Homer, whose Ulysses, says Lucian, evidently thought his hearers would swallow anything. In a Foreword to his story Lucian claims that "every episode is a subtle parody of some fantastic 'historic fact' recorded by an ancient poet, historian, or philosopher." Lucian thus originated a genre, that of the burlesque travel tale, of which the greatest example is no doubt *Gulliver's Travels*. The *True History* is also the first of numberless Trips to the Moon.

The racy translation, by Paul Turner, was published in 1958 by Indiana University Press and is reprinted by permission of Indiana University Press and Calder and Boyars Ltd.

I ONCE set sail from Gibraltar with a brisk wind behind and steered westward into the Atlantic. My reason for doing so? Mere curiosity. I just felt I needed a change, and wanted to find out what happened the other side of the Ocean, and what sort of people lived there. With this object in view I had taken on board an enormous supply of food and water, and collected fifty other young men who felt the same way as I did to keep me company. I had also provided all the weapons that we could possibly need, hired the best steersman available (at an exorbitant wage) and had our ship, which was only a light craft, specially reinforced to withstand the stresses and strains of a long voyage.

After sailing along at a moderate speed for twenty-four hours, we were still within sight of land; but at dawn the following day the wind increased to gale-force, the waves rose mountain-high, the sky grew black as night and it became impossible even to take in sail. There was nothing we could do but let her run before the wind and hope for the best.

The storm went on for seventy-nine days, but on the eightieth the sun suddenly shone through and revealed an island not far off. It was hilly and covered with trees, and now that the worst of the storm was over, the roar of the waves breaking against the shore had died down to a soft murmur. So we landed and threw ourselves down, utterly exhausted, on the sand. After all we had been through, you can imagine how long we lay there; but eventually we got up, and leaving thirty men to guard the ship, I and the other twenty went off to explore the island.

We started walking inland through the woods, and when we had gone about six hundred yards we came across a bronze tablet with a Greek inscription on it. The letters were almost worn away, but we just managed to make out the words: "Hercules and Dionysus got this far." We also spotted a couple of footprints on a rock nearby, one about a hundred feet long, and the other, I should say, about ninety-nine. Presumably Hercules has somewhat larger feet that Dionysus.

We sank reverently to our knees and said a prayer. Then we went on a bit further and came to a river of wine, which tasted exactly like Chianti. It was deep enough in places to float a battleship, and any doubts we might have

had about the authenticity of the inscription were immediately dispelled. Dionysus had been there all right!

I was curious to know where the river came from, so I
walked up-stream until I arrived at the source, which was
of a most unusual kind. It consisted of a group of giant
vines, loaded with enormous grapes. From the root of each
plant trickled sparkling drops of wine, which eventually
converged to form the river. There were lots of wine-col-
oured fish swimming about in it, and they tasted like wine
too, for we caught and ate some, and they made us extremely drunk. Needless to say, when we cut them open
we found they were full of wine-lees. Later, we hit on the
idea of diluting them with ordinary water-fish and thus
reducing the alcoholic content of our food.

After lunch we waded across the river at one of the
shallower spots, and came upon some specimens of a very
rare type of vine. They had good thick trunks growing out
of the ground in the normal manner, but apart from that
they were women, complete in every detail from the waist
upwards. In fact they were exactly like those pictures you
see of Daphne being turned into a tree just as Apollo is
about to catch her. From the tips of their fingers sprouted
vine-shoots loaded with grapes, and their hair consisted of
vine-leaves and tendrils.

When we went up to them, they shook us warmly by
the hand and said they were delighted to see us, some
saying it in Lydian, some in Hindustani, but most of them
in Greek. Then they wanted us to kiss them, and every
man who put his lips to theirs got very drunk and started
lurching about. They would not allow us to pick their
fruit, and shrieked with pain when anyone tried to do so;
but they were more than willing to be deflowered, and two

of us who volunteered to oblige them found it quite impossible to withdraw from their engagements afterwards.
They became literally rooted to the spot, their fingers
turning into vine-shoots and their hair into tendrils, and
looked like having little grapes of their own at the moment.

So we left them to their fate and ran back to the ship,
where we told the others what we had seen and described
the results of the experiment in cross-fertilisation. Then we
went off again with buckets to replenish our water-supply,
and while we were about it, to restock our cellar from the
river. After that we spent the night on the beach beside our
ship, and next morning put to sea with a gentle breeze
behind us.

About mid-day, when we had already lost sight of the
island, we were suddenly hit by a typhoon, which whirled
the ship round at an appalling speed and lifted it to a height
of approximately 1,800,000 feet. While we were up there, a
powerful wind caught our sails and bellied them out, so
instead of falling back on to the sea we continued to sail
through the air for the next seven days—and, of course, an
equal number of nights. On the eighth day we sighted what
looked like a big island hanging in mid-air, white and round
and brilliantly illuminated, so we steered towards it,
dropped anchor and disembarked.

A brief reconnaissance was enough to tell us that the
country was inhabited and under cultivation, and so long as
it was light that was all we could discover about our situation; but as soon as it got dark we noticed several other
flame-colored islands of various sizes in the vicinity, and far
below us we could see a place full of towns and rivers and
seas and forests and mountains, which we took to be the
Earth.

We decided to so some more exploring, but we had not

gone far before we were stopped and arrested by the local police. They are known in those parts as the Flying Squad, because they fly about on vultures, which they ride and control like horses. I should explain that the vultures in question are unusually large and generally have three heads. To give you some idea of their size, each of their feathers is considerably longer and thicker than the mast of a fairly large merchant-ship.

Now, one of the Flying Squad's duties is to fly about the country looking for undesirable aliens, and if it sees any to take them before the King. So that is what they did with us.

One glance at our clothes was enough to tell the King our nationality.

"Why, you're Greek, aren't you?" he said.

"Certainly we are," I replied.

"Then how on earth did you get here?" he asked. "How did you manage to come all that way through the air?"

So I told him the whole story, after which he told us his. It turned out that he came from Greece too, and was called Endymion. For some reason or other he had been whisked up here in his sleep and made King of the country, which was, he informed us, the Moon.

"But don't you worry," he went on. "I'll see you have everything you need. And if I win this war with Phaethon, you can settle down here quite comfortably for the rest of your lives."

"What's the war about?" I asked.

"Oh, it's been going on for ages," he answered. "Phaethon's my opposite number on the Sun, you know. It all started like this. I thought it would be a good idea to collect some of the poorer members of the community and send them off to form a colony on Lucifer, for it's completely uninhabited. Phaethon got jealous and despatched a contin-

gent of airborne troops, mounted on flying ants, to inter-
cept us when we were half-way there. We were hopelessly
outnumbered and had to retreat, but now I'm going to have
another shot at founding that colony, this time with full
military support. If you'd care to join the expedition, I'd be
only too glad to supply you with vultures from the royal
stables, and all other necessary equipment. We start first
thing tomorrow morning."

"Thanks very much," I said. "We'd love to come."

So he gave us an excellent meal and put us up for the
night, and early next morning assembled all his troops in
battle-formation, for the enemy were reported to be not far
off. The expeditionary force numbered a hundred thousand, exclusive of transport, engineers, infantry, and foreign auxiliaries, eight thousand being mounted on vultures,
and the other twenty on saladfowls. Saladfowls, incidentally, are like very large birds, except that they are fledged
with vegetables instead of feathers and have wings composed of enormous lettuce-leaves.

The main force was supported by a battery of Pea-shoot-
ers and a corps of Garlic-gassers, and also by a large contin-
gent of allies from the Great Bear, consisting of thirty
thousand Flea-shooters and fifty thousand Wind-jammers.
Flea-shooters are archers mounted on fleas—hence their
name—the fleas in question being approximately twelve
times the size of elephants. Wind-jammers are also airborne
troops, but they are not mounted on anything, nor do they
have any wings of their own. Their method of propulsion
is as follows: they wear extremely long night-shirts, which
belly out like sails in the wind and send them scudding
along like miniature ships through the air. Needless to say,
their equipment is usually very light.

In addition to all these, seventy thousand Sparrow-balls and fifty thousand Crane Cavalry were supposed to be arriving from the stars that shine over Cappadocia, but I did not see any of them, for they never turned up. In the circumstances I shall not attempt to describe what they were like—though I heard some stories about them which were really quite incredible.

All Endymion's troops wore the same type of equipment. Their helmets were made of beans, which grow very large and tough up there, and their bodies were protected by lupine seed-pods, stitched together to form a sort of armour-plate; for on the Moon these pods are composed of a horny substance which is practically impenetrable. As for their shields and swords, they were of the normal Greek pattern.

Our battle-formation was as follows. On the right wing were the troops mounted on vultures; among them was the King, surrounded by the pick of his fighting men, which included us. On the left wing were the troops mounted on saladfowls, and in the centre were the various allied contingents.

The infantry numbered approximately sixty million, and special steps had to be taken before they could be suitably deployed. There are, you must understand, large numbers of spiders on the Moon, each considerably larger than the average island in the Archipelago, and their services were requisitioned to construct a continuous cobweb between the Moon and Lucifer. As soon as the job had been done and the infantry had thus been placed on a firm footing, Nycterion, the third son of Eudianax, led them out on to the field of battle.

On the enemy's left wing was stationed the Royal Ant

Force, with Phaethon himself among them. These creatures looked exactly like ordinary flying ants, except for their enormous size, being anything up to two hundred feet long. They carried armed men on their backs, but with their huge antennae they did just as much of the fighting as their riders. They were believed to number about fifty thousand.

On the right wing were placed an equal number of Gnat-shooters, who were archers mounted on giant gnats. Behind them was a body of mercenaries from outer space. These were only light-armed infantry, but were very effective long-range fighters, for they bombarded us with colossal radishes, which inflicted foul-smelling wounds and caused instantaneous death. The explanation was said to be that the projectiles were smeared with a powerful toxin.

Next to the mercenaries were about ten thousand Mushroom Commandos, heavy-armed troops trained for hand-to-hand fighting who used mushrooms as shields and asparagus stalks as spears; and next to them again were five thousand Bow-wows from Sirius. These were dog-faced human beings mounted on flying chestnuts.

It was reported that Phaethon too had been let down by some of his allies, for an army of slingers was supposed to be coming from the Milky Way, and the Cloud-Centaurs had also promised their support. But the latter arrived too late for the battle (though far too soon for my comfort, I may add) and the slingers never turned up at all. Phaethon, I heard, was so cross about it that he went and burnt their milk for them shortly afterwards.

Eventually the signal-flags went up, there was a loud braying of donkeys on both sides—for donkeys are employed as trumpeters up there—and the battle began. The enemy's left wing immediately turned tail and fled, long before our vulture-riders had got anywhere near them, so we set off in pursuit and killed as many as we could. Their right wing, however, managed to break through our left one, and the Gnat-shooters came pouring through the gap until they were stopped by our infantry, who promptly made a counter-attack and forced them to retreat. Finally, when they realised that their left wing had already been beaten, the retreat became an absolute rout. We took vast numbers of prisoners, and killed so many men that the blood splashed all over the clouds and made them as red as a sunset. Quite a lot of it dripped right down on to the earth, and made me wonder if something of the sort had happened before, which would account for that extraordinary statement in Homer that Zeus rained down tears of blood at the thought of Sarpedon's death.

In the end we got tired of chasing them, so we stopped and erected two trophies, one in the middle of the cobweb to commemorate the prowess of the infantry, and one in the clouds to mark the success of our airborne forces. Just as we were doing so, a report came through that Phaethon's unpunctual allies, the Cloud-Centaurs, were rapidly approaching. When they finally appeared they were a most astonishing sight, for they were a cross between winged horses and human beings. The human part was about as big as the Colossus at Rhodes, and the horse-part was roughly the size of a large merchant-ship. I had better not tell you how many there were of them, for you would never believe me, if I did, but you may as well know that they were led by Sagittarius, the archer in the Zodiac.

Hearing that their allies had been defeated, they sent a message to Phaethon telling him to rally his forces and make a counter-attack. In the meantime they set the example by promptly spreading out in line and charging the Moon-people before they had time to organise themselves —for they had broken ranks as soon as the rout began, and now they were scattered about all over the place in search of loot. The result was that our entire army was put to flight, the King himself was chased all the way back to his capital, and most of his birds lost their lives.

The Cloud-Centaurs pulled down the trophies and devastated the whole cobweb, capturing me and two of my friends in the process. By this time Phaethon had returned to the scene of action and erected some trophies of his own, after which we were carried off to the Sun as prisoners of war, our hands securely lashed behind our backs with pieces of cobweb.

The victors decided not to besiege Endymion's capital, but merely to cut off his light-supply by building a wall in the middle of the air. The wall in question was composed of a double thickness of cloud, and was so effective that the Moon was totally eclipsed and condemned to a permanent state of darkness. Eventually Endymion was reduced to a policy of appeasement, and sent a message to Phaethon, humbly begging him to take down the wall and not make them spend the rest of their lives in the dark, volunteering to pay a war-indemnity and conclude a pact of non-aggression with the Sun, and offering hostages as a guarantee of his good faith.

Phaethon's Parliament met twice to consider these proposals. At the first meeting they passed a resolution rejecting them out of hand; at the second they reversed this decision, and agreed to make peace on terms which were ultimately incorporated in the following document:

An Agreement made this day between the Sun-people and their allies (hereinafter called *The Victors*) of the one part and the Moon-people and their allies (hereinafter called *The Vanquished*) of the other part

1. The Victors agree to demolish the wall, to refrain in future from invading the Moon, and to return their prisoners of war at a fixed charge per head.

2. The Vanquished agree not to violate the sovereign rights of other stars, and not to make war in future upon the Victors, but to assist them in case of attack by a third party, such assistance to be reciprocal.

3. The Vanquished undertake to pay to the Victors annually in advance ten thousand bottles of dew, and to commit ten thousand hostages to their keeping.

4. The colony on Lucifer shall be established jointly by both parties, other stars being free to participate if they so wish.

5. The terms of this agreement shall be inscribed on a column of amber, to be erected in the middle of the air on the frontier between the two kingdoms.

Signed for and on behalf of the Sun-people
and their allies

Rufus T. Fireman

for and on behalf of the Moon-people
and their allies

P. M. Loony

As soon as peace was declared, the wall was taken down and we three prisoners were released. When we got back to the Moon, we were greeted with tears of joy not only by the rest of our party but even by Endymion himself. He was very anxious for me to stay and help him with the colony, and actually offered to let me marry his son—for there are no such things as women on the Moon—but I was intent on getting down to the sea again, and as soon as he realised that I had made up my mind, he gave up trying to keep me. So off we went, after a farewell dinner which lasted for a week.

At this point I should like to tell you some of the odd things I noticed during my stay on the Moon. First of all, their methods of reproduction: as they have never even heard of women up there, the men just marry other men, and these other men have the babies. The system is that up to the age of twenty-five one acts as a wife, and from then on as a husband.

When a man is pregnant, he carries the child not in his stomach but in the calf of his leg, which grows extremely fat on these occasions. In due course they do a Caesarean, and the baby is taken out dead; but it is then brought to life by being placed in a high wind with its mouth wide open. Incidentally, it seems to me that these curious facts of lunar physiology may throw some light on a problem of etymology, for have we not here the missing link between the two apparently unconnected senses of the word *calf?*

Even more surprising is the method of propagating what are known as Tree-men. This is how it is done: you cut off the father's right testicle and plant it in the ground, where it grows into a large fleshy tree rather like a phallus, except that it has leaves and branches and bears fruit in the form of acorns, which are about eighteen inches long. When the fruit is ripe, it is picked and the babies inside are hatched out.

It is not uncommon up there to have artificial private parts, which apparently work quite well. If you are rich, you have them made of ivory, but the poorer classes have to rub along with wooden ones.

When Moon-people grow old, they do not die. They just vanish into thin air, like smoke—and talking of smoke, I must tell you about their diet, which is precisely the same for everyone. When they feel hungry, they light a fire and roast some frogs on it—for there are lots of these creatures flying about in the air. Then, while the frogs are roasting, they draw up chairs round the fire, as if it were a sort of dining-room table, and gobble up the smoke.

That is all they ever eat, and to quench their thirst they just squeeze some air into a glass and drink that: the liquid produced is rather like dew. They never make water in the other sense, nor do they ever evacuate their bowels, having no hole in that part of their anatomy; and if this makes you wonder what they do with their wives, the answer is that they have a hole in the crook of the knee, conveniently situated immediately above the calf.

Bald men are considered very handsome on the Moon, and long hair is thought absolutely revolting; but on young stars like the comets, which have not yet lost their hair, it is just the other way round—or so at least I was told by a Comet-dweller who was having a holiday on the Moon when I was there.

I forgot to mention that they wear their beards a little above the knee; and they have not any toe-nails, for the very good reason that they have not any toes. What they have got, however, is a large cabbage growing just above the buttocks like a tail. It is always in flower, and never gets broken, even if they fall flat on their backs.

When they blow their noses, what comes out is extremely sour honey, and when they have been working hard or taking strenuous exercise, they sweat milk at every pore. Occasionally they turn it into cheese, by adding a few drops of the honey. They also make olive-oil out of onions, and the resulting fluid is extremely rich and has a very delicate perfume.

They have any number of vines, which produce not wine but water, for the grapes are made of ice; and there, in my view, you have the scientific explanation of hail-storms, which occur whenever the wind is strong enough to blow the fruit off those vines.

They use their stomachs as handbags for carrying things around in, for they can open and shut them at will. If you look inside one, there is nothing to be seen in the way of digestive organs, but the whole interior is lined with fur so that it can also be used as a centrally-heated pram for babies in cold weather.

The upper classes wear clothes made of flexible glass, but this material is rather expensive, so most people have to be content with copper textiles—for there is any amount of copper in the soil, which becomes as soft as wool when soaked in water.

I hardly like to tell you about their eyes, for fear you should think I am exaggerating, because it really does sound almost incredible. Still, I might as well risk it, so here goes: their eyes are detachable, so that you can take them out when you do not want to see anything and put them back when you do. Needless to say, it is not unusual to find someone who has mislaid his own eyes altogether and is always having to borrow someone else's; and those who can afford it keep quite a number of spare pairs by them, just in case. As for ears, the Tree-men have wooden ones of their own, and everyone else has to be satisfied with a couple of plane-tree leaves instead.

I must just mention one other thing that I saw in the King's palace. It was a large mirror suspended over a fairly shallow tank. If you got into the tank, you could hear everything that was being said on the Earth, and if you looked in the mirror, you could see what was going on anywhere in the world, as clearly as if you were actually there yourself. I had a look at all the people I knew at home, but whether they saw me or not, I really cannot say.

Well, that is what it was like on the Moon. If you do not believe me, go and see for yourself.

DAPHNIS AND CHLOE
BY LONGUS

Of Longus we know absolutely nothing. We are not even sure of his name, which may be a misreading of the title of one manuscript of *Daphnis and Chloe*. At least provisionally, the story is dated about A.D. 200.

Daphnis and Chloe is the first pastoral romance, an idyll of awakening love in the hearts of simple, instinctive countryfolk, in a setting of flowers and balmy breezes. Kindly Nature acts as matchmaker. The story, rediscovered in the sixteenth century, started a centuries-long vogue for fluting love-sick shepherds and dainty shepherdesses, preserved now only in the form of Dresden china.

The anonymous translation was published by the Athenian Society of Athens in 1896. Here the story is much abridged by the editor.

[On the amorous island of Lesbos, Daphnis, a foundling, aged fifteen, tends his goats, in constant company with the thirteen-year-old shepherdess Chloe, also a foundling. They are fated to love; but their beauty and natural nobility are equaled by their innocence. A boorish but well-to-do herdsman, Dorcon, makes claim for Chloe's hand.]

I T WAS the end of spring and the commencement of summer: all Nature was in full vigour: the trees were full of fruit, the fields of corn. The chirp of the grasshopper was sweet to hear, the fruit sweet to smell, and the bleating of the sheep pleasant to the ear. The gently flowing rivers seemed to be singing a song: the winds, blowing softly through the pine-branches, sounded like the notes of the pipe: even the apples seemed to fall to the ground smitten with love, stripped off by the sun that was enamoured of their beauty. Daphnis, heated by all these surroundings, plunged into the river, sometimes to bathe, at other times to snare the fish that sported in the eddies of the stream: and he often drank, as if he could thereby quench the fire that consumed him. Chloe, after having milked her sheep and most of Daphnis's goats, was for a long time busied in curdling the milk: for the flies annoyed her terribly and stung her, when she endeavoured to drive them away. After this, she washed her face, and crowned with branches of pine, and girt with the skin of a fawn, filled a pail with wine and milk to share with Daphnis.

When noon came on, they were more enamoured than ever. For Chloe, having seen Daphnis quite naked, was struck by the bloom of his beauty, and her heart melted with love, for his whole person was too perfect for criticism: while Daphnis, seeing Chloe with her fawn skin and garland of pine, holding out the milkpail for him to drink, thought that he was gazing upon one of the Nymphs of the grotto. He snatched the garland from her head, kissed it, and placed it on his own: and Chloe took his clothes when he had stripped to bathe, kissed them, and in like manner put them on. Sometimes they pelted each other with apples, and parted and decked each other's hair. Chloe declared that Daphnis's hair, being dark, was like myrtle berries: while Daphnis compared Chloe's face to an apple, because it was fair and ruddy. He also taught her to play on the pipe: and, when she began to blow, he snatched it away, and ran over the reeds with his lips: and, while he thus pretended to show her where she was wrong, he speciously kissed the pipe in the places where her mouth had been.

While he was piping in the noonday heat, and the flocks were resting in the shade, Chloe unwittingly fell asleep. When Daphnis perceived this, he put down his pipe, and gazed at her all over with greedy eyes, without any feeling of shame, and at the same time gently whispered to himself: "How lovely are her eyes in sleep! how sweet the perfume from her mouth, sweeter than that of apples or the hawthorn! Yet I dare not kiss it: her kiss pricks me to the heart, and maddens me like fresh honey. Besides, if I kiss her, I am afraid of waking her. O chattering grasshoppers! you will prevent her from sleeping, if you chirp so loudly! And on the other side, the he-goats are butting each other with their horns: O wolves, more cowardly than foxes, why do you not carry them off?"

While he was thus talking to himself, a grasshopper, pursued by a swallow, fell into Chloe's bosom: the swallow followed, but could not catch it: but, being unable to check its flight, touched Chloe's cheek with its wing. Not knowing what was the matter, she cried out loudly, and woke up with a start: but, when she saw the swallow flying close to her, and Daphnis laughing at her alarm, she was reassured, and rubbed her still drowsy eyes. The grasshopper, as if in gratitude for its safety, chirped its thanks from her bosom. Then Chloe cried out again, and Daphnis laughed: and, seizing the opportunity, thrust his hand into her breast, and pulled out the grateful insect, which continued its song, even while held a prisoner in his hand. Chloe was delighted, and having kissed the insect, took it and put it, still chirping, into her bosom.

Another time, they were listening with delight to the cooing of a wood-pigeon. When Chloe asked what was the meaning of its song, Daphnis told her the popular story: "Once upon a time, dear maiden, there was a maiden, beautiful and blooming as yourself. She tended cattle and sang beautifully: her cows were so enchanted by the music of her voice, that she never needed to strike them with her crook or to touch them with her goad: but, seated beneath a pine tree, her head crowned with a garland, she sang of Pan and Pinus, and the cows stood near, enchanted by her song. There was a young man who tended his flocks hard by, beautiful and a good singer himself, as she was, who entered into a rivalry of song with her: his voice was more powerful, since he was a man, and yet gentle, since he was but a youth. He sang so sweetly that he charmed eight of her best cows and enticed them over to his own herd, and drove them away. The maiden, grieved at the loss of her cattle, and at having been vanquished in singing, begged the Gods to transform her into a bird before she returned home. The Gods listened to her prayer, and transformed her into a mountain bird, which loves to sing as she did. Even now it tells in plaintive tones of her misadventure, and how that she is still seeking the cows that strayed away."

Such were the enjoyments which the summer afforded them. But, in mid-autumn, when the grapes grew ripe, some Tyrian pirates, having embarked on a light Carian vessel, that they might not be suspected of being barbarians, landed on the coast: and, armed with swords and corslets, carried off everything that came into their hands, fragrant wine, a great quantity of wheat, and honey in the honey-comb, besides some cows belonging to Dorcon. They also seized Daphnis as he was wandering on the shore: for Chloe, being a simple girl, for fear of the insolence of the shepherds, did not drive out the flocks of Dryas so early. When the robbers beheld the tall and handsome youth, a more valuable booty than any they could find in the fields, they paid no heed to the goats or the other fields, but carried him off to their ship, weeping and in great distress what to do, and calling the while for Chloe in a loud voice.

No sooner had they loosed the cable, and begun to ply their oars, and put out to sea, than Chloe drove down her flock, bringing with her a new pipe as a present to Daphnis. But, seeing the goats scattered hither and thither, and hearing Daphnis calling to her ever louder and louder, thinking no more about her sheep, she flung away the pipe, and ran to Dorcon, to implore his aid.

She found him lying prostrate on the ground, hacked by the swords of the robbers, and almost dead from loss of blood. But, when he saw Chloe, revived by the smouldering fire of his former passion, he said: "Chloe, dear, I am at the point of death: when I tried to defend my cattle, the accursed brigands hewed me to pieces like an ox. But do you save Daphnis for yourself: avenge me, and destroy them. I have taught my cows to follow the sound of the pipe, and to come when they hear it, however far off they may be feeding. Come, take this pipe, and play the same strain upon it which I once taught Daphnis, and he in turn taught you. Leave the rest to my pipe and my cows that are on yonder ship. I also make you a present of the pipe, with which I have gained the victory over many herdsmen and shepherds. Kiss me once in return, and lament for me when I am dead: and, when you see another tending my cattle, then think of me."

When Dorcon had thus spoken, and had kissed her for the last time, he breathed his last as he spoke and kissed her. Chloe took the pipe, put it to her lips, and blew with all her might. And the cows heard it, and, recognising the strain, began to low, and all with a bound sprang into the sea. As they had leaped from the same side of the vessel, and caused the sea to part, it upset and sank under the waves that closed over it. Those on board were flung into the sea, but with unequal prospect of safety. For the pirates were encumbered with swords, and clad in scaly coats of mail, and greaves reaching halfway down the leg. But Daphnis, who had been tending his flocks, was unshod, and only half-clothed, owing to the burning heat. The pirates had only swum a little way, when the weight of their armour dragged them down into the depths: Daphnis easily threw off the clothes he had on, yet it cost him some effort to swim, since he had hitherto only swum in rivers: but soon, under the impulse of necessity, he reached the cows by an effort, and, while with each hand he grasped one by the horns, he was carried along between them without difficulty or danger, as if he had been driving a cart: for an ox swims far better than any man: it is only inferior to the water-fowl and fishes. An ox would never sink, were it not that the horn falls off their hoofs when it gets wet through. The truth of what I say is borne out by many places on the coast which are still found bearing the name of "Oxfords."

Thus Daphnis, against all expectation, was saved from the double danger of the robbers and shipwreck. When he came to land, and found Chloe weeping and smiling through her tears, he threw himself into her arms, and asked her what she had meant by playing on the pipe. And she told him everything, how she had run to Dorcon for help, how his cows had been trained to obey the sound of the pipe, what strain she had been bidden to play, and how Dorcon had died: only, from a feeling of modesty, she said nothing about the kiss she had given him. Then both resolved to honour the memory of their benefactor, and went with his relatives to bury the unhappy Dorcon. They heaped earth over him in abundance, and planted a number of cultivated trees round about, and hung up as an offering to the deceased the first fruits of their labours: they poured libations of milk over his grave, crushed grapes, and broke several shepherds' pipes. His cows lowed piteously, wandering hither and thither the while: and to the herdsmen and shepherds it seemed that they were mourning for the death of their master.

After the burial of Dorcon, Chloe led Daphnis to the grotto of the Nymphs, where she washed him, and then she herself, for the first time in Daphnis's presence, also washed her own fair and beautiful person, which needed no bath to set off its beauty: then, plucking the flowers that were in season, they crowned the statues of the Nymphs, and hung up Dorcon's pipe against the rock as an offering. After this, they went to look after their sheep and goats, which were all lying on the ground, neither feeding nor bleating, but, I believe, pining for the absent Daphnis and Chloe. But, as soon as they came in sight, and began to shout and pipe as usual, they jumped up and began to feed: the goats skipped wantonly, as if delighted at the safe return of their master. Daphnis however could not bring himself to feel happy: for, since he had seen Chloe naked, in all her beauty formerly hidden and then revealed, he felt a pain in his heart, as if it was consumed by poison. His breath now came rapidly, as if someone was pursuing him: and now failed him, as if exhausted in previous attacks. Chloe's bath seemed to him more terrible than the sea. He thought that his soul was still amongst the pirates, since he was merely a young rustic and as yet knew nothing of the thievish tricks of Love.

It was soon the middle of autumn, and the vintage was close at hand; everyone was in the fields, busily intent upon his work. Some were repairing the wine-presses, others cleaning out the jars: some were weaving baskets of osier, and others sharpening short sickles for cutting the grapes: some were preparing stones to crush the juicy grapes, others preparing dry twigs which had been well beaten, to be used as torches to light the drawing off of the new wine by night. Daphnis and Chloe, having abandoned the care of their flocks, assisted each other in these tasks. Daphnis carried bunches of grapes in baskets, threw them into the press and trod them, and drew off the juice into jars: while Chloe prepared food for the vintagers, and poured some of the older wine for them to drink, while at the same time she picked some of the lowest branches from the trees. For all the vines in Lesbos grow low, and are not trained to trees: their branches hang down to the ground, spreading like ivy, so that even a child that is, so to speak, only just out of its swaddling clothes, could reach them.

As is customary at the festival of Bacchus, on the birthday of the wine, women had been summoned from the neighbouring fields to assist; and they cast amorous eyes on Daphnis, and extolled him as vying with Bacchus in beauty. One of them, bolder than the rest, kissed him, which excited Daphnis, but annoyed Chloe. On the other hand, the men who were treading the wine-presses made all kinds of advances to Chloe, and leaped furiously, like Satyrs who had seen some Bacchante, declaring that they wished they were sheep, to be tended by her: this, again, pleased Chloe, while Daphnis felt annoyed. Each wished that the vintage was over, and that they could return to the familiar fields, and, instead of uncouth shouts, hear the sound of the pipe and the bleating of their flocks.

In a few days the grapes were gathered in, the casks were full of new wine, and there was no need of so many hands: then they again began to drive their flocks down to the plain, and joyfully paid homage to the Nymphs, offering them grapes still hanging on the branches, the first fruits of the vintage. Even before that they had never neglected them as they passed by, but when they drove their flocks to pasture, as well as on their return, they reverently saluted them; never omitting to bring them a flower, some fruit, some green foliage, or a libation of milk. And they afterward reaped the reward of this piety from the Gods. Then they gamboled like dogs loosed from their bonds, piped, sang to the goats, and wrestled sportively with the sheep.

[An old man, Philetas, tells Daphnis and Chloe that he has seen the God of Love hovering near. He concludes: "You are consecrated to Love, my children, and Love watches over you."]

Daphnis and Chloe were as delighted as if they had heard some fable, and not a true story, and asked what Love was; whether it was a bird or a child, and what it could do. Philetas replied: "My children, Love is a winged God, young and beautiful. Wherefore he takes delight in youth, pursues beauty, and furnishes the soul with wings: his power is greater than that of Zeus. He has power over the elements and over the stars: and has greater control over the other Gods that are his equals than you have over your sheep and goats. The flowers are all the work of Love; the plants are his creation. He makes the rivers to run, and the winds to blow. I have seen a bull smitten with love, and it bellowed as if stung by the gadfly: I have seen a he-goat kissing its mate, and following it everywhere. I myself have been young, and was in love with Amaryllis: then I thought neither of eating nor drinking, and I took no rest. My soul was troubled, my heart beat, my body was chilled: I shouted as if I were being beaten, I was as silent as a dead man, I plunged into the rivers as if I were consumed by fire: I called upon Pan, himself enamoured of Pitys, to help me: I thanked Echo, who repeated the name of Amaryllis after me: I broke my pipes, which, though they charmed my kine, could not bring Amaryllis to me. For there is no remedy for Love, that can be eaten or drunk, or uttered in song, save kissing and embracing, and lying naked side by side."

Philetas, having thus instructed them, departed, taking away with him a present of some cheeses and a horned goat. When they were left alone, having then for the first time heard the name of Love, they were greatly distressed, and, on their return to their home at night, compared their feelings with what they had heard from the old man: "Lovers suffer: so do we. They neglect their work: we have done the same. They cannot sleep: it is the same with us. They seem on fire: we are consumed by fire. They are eager to see each other: it is for this that we wish the day to dawn more quickly. This must be Love, and we are in love with each other without knowing it. If this be not love, and I am not beloved, why are we so distressed? why do we so eagerly seek each other? All that Philetas has told us is true. It was that boy in the garden who once appeared to our parents in a dream, and bade us tend the flocks. How can we catch him? he is small and will escape. And how can we escape him? he has wings and will overtake us. We must appeal to the Nymphs for help. But Pan could not help Philetas, when he was in love with Amaryllis. Let us, therefore, try the remedies of which he told us: let us kiss and embrace each other, and lie naked on the ground. It is cold: but we will endure it, after the example of Philetas."

This was their nightly lesson. At daybreak they drove out their flocks, kissed each other as soon as they met, which they had never done before, and embraced: but they were afraid to try the third remedy, to undress and lie down together: for it would have been too bold an act for a young shepherdess, even for a goatherd. Then again they passed sleepless nights, thinking of what they had done, and regretting what they had left undone. "We have kissed each other," they complained, "but it has profited nothing. We have embraced, but nothing has come of it. The only remaining remedy is to lie down together: let us try it: surely there must be something in it more efficacious than in a kiss."

With such thoughts as these their dreams were naturally of love and kisses and embraces: what they had not done in the day, they did in a dream: they lay naked together. The next morning, they got up more inflamed with love then ever, and drove their flocks to pasture, whistling loudly, and hurried to embrace each other: and, when they saw each other from a distance, they ran up with a smile, kissed, and embraced: but the third remedy was slow to come: for Daphnis did not venture to speak of it, and Chloe was unwilling to lead the way, until chance brought them to it.

They were sitting side by side on the trunk of an oak: and, having tasted the delights of kissing, they could not have enough: in their close embrace their lips met closely. While Daphnis pulled Chloe somewhat roughly towards him, she somehow fell on her side, and Daphnis, following up his kiss, fell also on his side: then, recognising the likeness of the dream, they lay for a long time as if they had been bound together. But, not knowing what to do next, and thinking that this was the consummation of love, they spent the greater part of the day in these idle embraces; then, cursing the night when it came on, they separated, and drove their flocks home. Perhaps they would have found out the truth, had not a sudden disturbance occupied the attention of the whole district.

[Some wealthy young men of a neighboring city cruise the coast, hunting and fishing. Their boat is carried out to sea;

Daphnis is wrongfully blamed. The incident provokes a war. The invaders carry off Chloe. She is miraculously saved by Pan and the Nymphs. Winter, confining the flocks, parts the lovers.]

With the commencement of spring the snow began to melt, the earth again became visible, and the green grass sprouted. The shepherds again drove their flocks into the fields, Daphnis and Chloe first of all, since they served a mightier shepherd. They ran first to the grotto of the Nymphs, then to the pine tree and the image of Pan, and after that to the oak, under which they sat down, watching their flocks and kissing each other. Then, to weave chaplets for the Gods, they went in search of some flowers, which were only just beginning to blossom under the fostering influence of Zephyr and the warmth of the sun: however, they found some violets, hyacinths, pimpernel, and other flowers of early spring. After they had drunk some new milk drawn from the sheep and goats, they crowned the images, and poured libations. Then they began to play upon their pipes, as if challenging to song the nightingales, which were warbling in the thickets and gradually perfecting their lamentation for Itys, as if anxious, after long silence, to recall their strains.

The sheep began to bleat, the lambs gamboled, or stooped under their mothers' bellies to suck their teats. The rams chased the sheep which had not yet borne young, and mounted them. The he-goats also chased the she-goats with even greater heat, leaped amorously upon them, and fought for them. Each had his own mate, and jealously guarded her against the attacks of a wanton rival. At this sight even old men would have felt the fire of love rekindled within them: the more so Daphnis and Chloe, who were young and tortured by desire, and had long been in quest of the delights of love. All that they heard inflamed them, all that they saw melted them, and they longed for something more than mere embraces and kisses, but especially Daphnis, who, having spent the winter in the house doing nothing, kissed Chloe fiercely, pressed her wantonly in his arms, and showed himself in every respect more curious and audacious.

He begged her to grant him all he desired, and to lie with him naked longer than they had been accustomed to do: "This," said he, "is the only one of Philetas's instructions that we have not yet followed, the only remedy that can appease Love." When Chloe asked him what else there could be besides kisses, embraces, and lying together, and what he meant to do, if they both lay naked together, he replied: "The same as the rams and the he-goats do to their mates. You see how, after this has been accomplished, the former no longer pursue the latter, nor the latter flee from the former: but, from that moment, they feed quietly together, as if they had enjoyed the same pleasure in common. This pastime, methinks, is something sweet, which can overcome the bitterness of love." "But," answered Chloe, "do you not see that he-goats and she-goats, rams and sheep, all satisfy their desire standing upright: the males leap upon the females, who receive them on their backs? You ask me to lie down with you naked: but see how much thicker their fleece is than my garments." Daphnis obeyed, lay down by her side, and held her for a long time clasped in his arms: but, not knowing how to do what he was burning to do, he made her get up, and embraced her behind, in imitation of the he-goats, but with even less success: then, utterly at a loss what to do, he sat down on the ground and began to weep at the idea of being more ignorant of the mysteries of love than the rams.

In the neighbourhood there dwelt a labourer named Chromis, already advanced in years, who farmed his own estate. He had a wife whom he had brought from the city, young, beautiful, and more refined than the country-women: her name was Lycaenium. Every morning she saw Daphnis driving his goats to pasture, and back again at night. She was seized with a desire of winning him for her lover by presents. Having watched until he was alone, she gave him a pipe, a honeycomb, and a deer-skin wallet, but she was afraid to say anything, suspecting his love for Chloe. For she had observed that he was devoted to the girl, although hitherto she had only guessed his affection from having seen them interchange nods and smiles. One day, in the morning, making the excuse to Chromis that she was going to visit a neighbour who had been brought to bed, she followed them, concealed herself in a thicket to avoid being seen, and heard all they said, and saw all they did. Even Daphnis's tears did not escape her. Pitying the poor young couple, and thinking that she had a two-fold oppor-tunity—of getting them out of their trouble and, at the same time, satisfying her own desires, she had recourse to the following stratagem.

The next day, having gone out again on pretence of visiting her sick neighbour, she proceeded straight to the oak under which Daphnis and Chloe were sitting, and, pretending to be in great distress, cried: "Help me, Daphnis: I am most unhappy. An eagle has just carried off the finest of my twenty geese: but, as the burden was a heavy one, he could not carry it up to the top of the rock, his usual refuge, but has alighted with his prey at the end of the wood. In the name of the Nymphs and Pan yonder, I beseech you, go with me into the forest, for I am afraid to go alone: save my goose, and do not leave the number of my flock imperfect. Perhaps you will also be able to slay the eagle, and he will no longer carry off your kids and lambs. Meanwhile, Chloe can look after your goats: they know her as well as you: for you always tend your flocks together."

Daphnis, suspecting nothing of what was to come, immediately got up, took his crook and followed Lycaenium. She took him as far from Chloe as possible, and, when they came to the thickest part of the forest, she bade him sit down near a fountain, and said: "Daphnis, you are in love with Chloe: the Nymphs revealed this to me last night. They told me in a dream of the tears you shed yesterday, and bade me relieve you of your trouble by teaching you the mysteries of love. These consist not in kisses and embraces alone, or the practices of sheep and goats, but in connexion far more delightful than these: for the pleasure lasts longer. If then you wish to be freed from your troubles and to try the delights of which you are in search, come, put yourself in my hands, a delightful pupil: out of gratitude to the Nymphs, I will be your instructress."

Daphnis, at these words, could no longer contain himself for joy: but, being a simple countryman and goatherd, young and amorous, he threw himself at her feet and begged her to teach him without delay the art which would enable him to do to Chloe what he desired: and, as if it had been some profound and heaven-sent secret, he promised to give her a kid lately weaned, fresh cheeses made of new milk, and even the mother herself. Lycaenium seeing, from his generous offer, that Daphnis was more simple than she had imagined, began to instruct him in the following manner. She ordered him to sit down by her side just as he was, and to kiss her as he had been accustomed to kiss Chloe, and, while kissing, to embrace her and lie down by her side.

When he had done so, Lycaenium, finding that he was ready for action and inflamed with desire, lifted him up a little, and, cleverly slipping under him, set him on the road he had sought so long in vain: and, without more ado, Nature herself taught him the rest.

[After many adventures and misadventures Daphnis and Chloe find their parents, who are of course rich and eminent. Their marriage is at last formally celebrated.]

As it was a very fine day, Dionysophanes [Daphnis' father] ordered couches of green leaves to be spread in front of the grotto, invited all the villagers to the festivities, and entertained them handsomely. . . . All the amusements were of a rustic and pastoral character, as was natural, considering the guests. One sang a reaper's song, another repeated the jests of the vintage season. . . . The goats also were feeding close at hand, as if they desired to take part in the banquet. This was not altogether to the taste of the city people: but Daphnis called some of them by name, gave them some green leaves to eat, took them by the horns and kissed them.

And not only then, but as long as they lived, they devoted most of their time to a pastoral life. They paid especial reverence to the Nymphs, Pan, and Love, acquired large flocks of goats and sheep, and considered fruit and milk superior to every other kind of food. When a son was born to them, they put him to suck a goat: their daughter was suckled by a ewe: and they called the former Philopoemen, and the latter Agele. Thus they lived to a good old age in the fields, decorated the grotto, set up statues, and erected an altar to Shepherd Love, and, in place of the pine, built a temple for Pan to dwell in, and dedicated it to Pan the Soldier.

But this did not take place until later. After the banquet, when night came, all the guests accompanied them to the nuptial chamber, playing on the pipe and flute, and carrying large blazing torches. When they were near the door, they began to sing in a harsh and rough voice, as if they were breaking up the earth with forks, instead of singing the marriage hymn. Daphnis and Chloe, lying naked side by side, embraced and kissed each other, more wakeful than the owl, the whole night long. Daphnis put into practice the lessons of Lycaenium, and then for the first time Chloe learned that all that had taken place between them in the woods was nothing more than the childish amusement of shepherds.

AN ETHIOPIAN STORY
BY HELIODORUS

According to Heliodorus' own statement at the end of his *Aethiopica*, he was a Phoenician, of the family of hereditary priests of the sun, and resided in Emesa, the present Homs in Syria, not far from the Mediterranean coast. His book may be dated in the second or third centuries A.D.; one good guess is the year 230. It is an adventure story of lovers at odds with all the efforts of fate and circumstance to part them. The interest of the reader is engaged by the variety of the incidents and by the local color more than by the characters, who were stock figures even in their own time.

Most of the first chapter is given here. The translation, anonymous, was published by the Athenian Society of Athens in 1897.

THE LIGHT of day had just begun to smile and the rays of the sun to illumine the mountain ridges, when some armed men, whose attire proclaimed them brigands, showed themselves on the top of a promontory which overhangs the outlet of the Nile, which is called the Hercules mouth; there they halted for a while, carefully examining the expanse of sea that lay beneath them. Having first cast their eyes over the open and seeing no vessel that held out hopes of plunder, they turned their gaze towards the beach, where they beheld the following sight:

A vessel was lying at anchor; there was no one on board, but it carried a heavy cargo, as could be guessed even by those at a distance; for the weight of it caused the ship to sink in the water as high as the third band. The whole beach was covered with bodies of men but lately massacred, some quite dead, others still alive, their limbs yet quivering, which proved that a fierce struggle had just ended. But the indications were not those of a regular battle; with the dead and dying were mingled the miserable remains of an ill-starred feast, which had had so disastrous an issue; tables still covered with viands, fragments of others still clutched in the hands of the dead, who had used them as weapons in the sudden outburst of the fray, while others again, to all appearance, had been used as hiding-places; drinking-cups lying on the ground, some of which had fallen from the hands of the banqueters who had been slain in the act of lifting them to their mouth, while others had been used as stones. The suddenness of the attack had invented new uses for them and taught the combatants to use cups in place of weapons. One lay wounded by an axe, another with his brains dashed out by stones picked up from the beach; one had been battered to pieces with a club, another scorched by the fire of a blazing torch; death had overtaken them in various ways, but most of them had been pierced with arrows. Fortune had gathered together in a small space a countless variety of objects, polluting wine with blood, uniting war and festivity, and mingling promiscuously drinking and death, libations and slaughter. Such was the sight she set before the eyes of the Egyptian brigands.

The latter, spectators from the top of the mountain, were unable to understand the scene; they beheld numbers overthrown, but could not see their conquerors; all the signs of a brilliant victory, but the spoils untouched; a vessel without a crew, but in other respects uninjured, as if it were strongly defended or were tossing quietly at anchor. Although they did not know what had happened, the greed of gain excited them, and, as if they had been themselves the conquerors, they proceeded to descend, in order to lay hands upon the plunder.

When they were only a short distance from the vessel

and the bodies of the dead and dying, another sight, which perplexed them even more, arrested their attention. They saw a young girl, of wondrous beauty, sitting on a rock, whom they took to be a goddess; though smitten with grief at the scene, her mien and features displayed a dignified and noble spirit; her head was crowned with laurel, a quiver was slung over her shoulders, her left arm rested upon her bow, while the hand hung carelessly down; with her right elbow resting upon her thigh, she leaned her cheek upon her hand, with head bent, looking from time to time at a young man lying a little distance from her on the shore.

This young man, covered with cruel wounds, with difficulty managed to lift up his head from a deep sleep, that resembled the sleep of death. But, even in this plight, a manly beauty shone upon his face; the blood, trickling down his cheeks, enhanced the charm of his fair complexion. But pain and grief, in spite of all his efforts, drew down his eyelids, while, on the other hand, the sight of the maiden attracted his gaze, and his eyes were constrained to look, because they saw her. At last he recovered himself, and, heaving a deep sigh, cried in a feeble voice: "My dearest, are you really preserved to me? or have you too been slain amongst the rest? has not even death been able to separate us, that your shade and spirit still accompany my fortunes?" "My destiny, my life or death, is bound up with yours," replied the young girl; "you see this (here she showed him a dagger on her knees); if it has hitherto remained idle, it has only been held back by the signs of life in you." With these words, she sprang up from the rock. The spectators on the mountain, smitten with wonder and amazement, as if they had been struck by lightning, ran to shelter themselves beneath the bushes; for, when she stood up, she appeared even taller and more divine. The arrows in

her quiver, which her sudden movements caused to rattle
on her shoulders, the dazzling brilliancy of her gold-be-
decked robe which glittered in the rays of the sun, her long
hair which floated from beneath her crown like that of a
Bacchante, hanging half-way down her back, and, more
than what they saw, their ignorance of what had taken
place—all this struck terror into their souls.

"She is a goddess," cried some, "either Artemis or Isis,
the divine patroness of Egypt"; while others declared that
she was some priestess inspired with divine frenzy, who had
wrought such slaughter. Such was their opinion; but as yet
they knew not the truth.

Meanwhile, the young girl hastened to the youth, flung
her arms around him, wept and kissed him, wiped off the
blood, uttered loud groans, and, although she held him in
her grasp, seemed scarcely able to believe her eyes. When
the Egyptians saw this, they altered their opinion. "How,"
said they, "can this be the act of a goddess? Would she
embrace a lifeless corpse so affectionately?" After this, they
encouraged one another to take heart, and draw nearer and
learn the truth. Their courage revived, they descended, and
found the young girl still tending the other's wounds;
standing behind, they remained motionless, venturing
neither to speak nor to act. The girl, hearing the noise of
their footsteps and seeing their shadows on the ground,
looked up; in no way alarmed by their strange complexion,
or their arms, which proclaimed them brigands, she low-
ered her eyes again, and devoted her whole attention to the
prostrate youth. Thus the keenness of regret and the sincer-
ity of love make us disregard all external objects whether
pleasant or painful, and compel us to see nothing but the
one beloved object, and to devote to it our whole attention.

When the brigands stopped in front of her, apparently

intending to lay hands on her, she looked up again, and, seeing their dark complexions and hideous appearance, thus addressed them:

"If you are the shades of the dead that are lying here, you do wrong to trouble us; for most of you have died by your own hands; those who were slain by us deserved their fate; we only exercised the right of self-defence to protect our honour. If you are living men, you would seem to be brigands; then you have arrived at a fitting moment to deliver us from our present calamities, and to end this scene of horror by our death."

Such was the tragic plaint she uttered. The others, unable to understand what she said, left the unhappy pair, thinking their weakness a sufficient guard; then, hurrying to the ship, they ransacked the cargo, which was considerable and consisted of various kinds of wares; to some they paid no heed, but carried off gold and silver, precious stones, and silken stuffs, as much as they could carry. When their greed was satisfied, they spread the booty on the shore, and divided it into equal portions, making the distribution not according to the value, but by the weight of each article. They had decided to defer the consideration of what they should do with their prisoners.

Meanwhile, another band of brigands came up, with two horsemen riding at their head. When the first band perceived them, without venturing to show fight or carry off any portion of the booty, for fear they might be pursued, they fled with all speed, being only ten in number, while those whom they saw coming were three times as many. Thus the young girl found herself captured a second time, although not actually a prisoner. The new arrivals, although intent on plunder, halted for a while, astounded at what they saw and ignorant of the cause. They imagined that those who had just fled had perpetrated the massacre, and seeing that the young girl, dressed in strange and magnificent attire, paid no attention to the dangers that threatened her, as if they had no existence, but devoted all her care to the young man's wounds, and seemed to feel his sufferings as if they were her own, they stood still, struck with admiration at her beauty and courageous spirit, while they were equally astonished at the form and stature of the wounded young man, who had gradually recovered, while his features resumed their ordinary expression.

At length the captain of the band drew near, laid his hand upon the young girl, and commanded her to get up and follow him. Guessing what he meant (although she did not understand his words), she began to drag the young man along with her, who himself refused to part from her; then, pointing the dagger towards her breast, she threatened to kill herself, unless they took him as well. Her gestures, rather than her words, explained her meaning to the Captain, who, hoping that the young man, if he recovered, might be of great service to him, dismounted and ordered his esquire to do the same, and bade his prisoners mount in their places. Bidding his men collect the spoil and follow him, he himself walked on foot by the side of the captives, to hold them up in case they should be in danger of falling. Nor was their lot without its compensation; the master seemed to be the slave, and the captor the servant of the captured. So true is it that the appearance of nobility and the sight of beauty are able to subjugate even the hearts of brigands and to conquer the harshest natures.

After the brigands had followed the coast for a distance of about two furlongs, they left the sea on their right, and turned aside in the direction of a mountain, which they climbed with difficulty, and, descending the other side with all speed, arrived at a lake which lay below. The whole district is called Bucolia (Pasture) by the Egyptians. In it there is a valley, which receives the overflow of the Nile and becomes a lake, very deep in the middle, while its shores are shallow and marshy; for the waters of lakes, like those of the sea, diminish in depth the nearer they are to the land. This spot is as it were the republic of all the brigands of Egypt. Some dwell in huts which they have built upon rising ground above the level of the water, while others live in boats, which they use both for habitation and purposes of transport; it is here that their wives spin, and are brought to bed. Their children are first brought up on their mothers' milk, afterwards upon fish caught in the lake and dried in the sun. As soon as a child can crawl, a cord is tied to its ankles and it is allowed to go as far as the edge of the boat or the door of the hut, the cord being used as a guide.

Thus those who are born on the lake look upon it as their nurse and native land, and regard it as a safe stronghold for brigands like themselves, who flock thither in large numbers. The water serves them as a wall, and the reeds, which grow in abundance, as a palisade. Amongst these reeds they have cut several winding and tortuous paths, easy for themselves to find who know them, but which are difficult of access to others and form a strong defence against invasion. Such is this little republic, and such the manners of its inhabitants.

The sun was setting when the captain and his followers reached the lake. They made the prisoners dismount, and put the booty on board the boats. Those who had not taken part in the expedition issued in large numbers from different sides of the marsh, and hurried to meet their chief, whom they received with as much reverence as if he had been a king. At the sight of the rich spoil and the divine beauty of the maiden, they imagined that some temple or shrine had been plundered by their companions, thinking, in their rustic simplicity, that they had carried off the priestess or the breathing image of some goddess. Then, with loud praises and congratulations, they escorted their chief in triumph to his abode.

This was a small island, apart from the rest, which he shared with a small number of intimate friends. As soon as he arrived there, he bade the multitude return home, after having ordered them all to assemble before him on the following day. He himself, with a few intimate friends, took a hasty supper, and then handed over the young couple to a young Greek, who had been taken prisoner by the brigands a short time before, that he might serve as interpreter; he lodged them in part of his own hut, and charged the Greek to pay careful attention to the young man, and, above all, to see that no insult was offered to the young lady. He himself, exhausted by the fatigues of his journey, and overwhelmed with the anxieties of command, soon fell asleep.

When silence reigned throughout the marsh, about the first watch of the night, the maiden took advantage of the solitude and the absence of those who were likely to disturb her, to give vent to her sorrow; the quiet of the night only increased her grief, since nothing was to be seen or heard that could divert her painful thoughts. Separated from the rest by the captain's order, and lying upon a miserable couch, she sighed and shed bitter tears: "O Apollo, how cruel is the punishment you inflict upon us, far greater than our offences deserve! Is not your vengeance satisfied with the misfortunes which we have already suffered? Deprived of our parents, captured by pirates, exposed to perils without number on the sea, a second time fallen into the hands of brigands—can worse than this await us? when will you put an end to our miseries? Provided I could die pure and without reproach, death would be welcome. But if anyone should dare to attempt to obtain by force the favours which even my Theagenes has never obtained, I would strangle myself and forestall the crime; so would I keep myself pure and chaste, as I have hitherto done, even to the hour of death, and virtue itself should be my honourable shroud. No judge will ever be more pitiless than you, O Apollo!"

She would have proceeded, but Theagenes interrupted her: "Hush, my life, my dearest Chariclea! your laments are just, but they provoke the god more than you imagine. You must not reproach him, but invoke his aid. Prayers are more likely than accusations to appease the wrath of those who are mightier than ourselves." "You are right," she replied: "but, tell me, I beg you, how are you yourself?" "Better, since evening; this young man's attention has allayed the inflammation of my wounds." "You will find yourself much easier in the morning," rejoined their keeper: "I will apply a certain herb to your wounds, which in three days will heal them. I know its valuable properties by experience. Since I have been a prisoner here, when any of the Captain's followers return wounded from an expedition, I apply this remedy, which soon restores them to health. Do not be surprised if I sympathize with you; your lot seems to resemble mine; besides, since I myself am a Greek, I cannot help pitying you who are Greeks." "A Greek! Oh, heavens!" exclaimed the youthful pair, transported with joy. "Yes, most assuredly: a Greek both by birth and language." "Perhaps we shall obtain some alleviation of our sorrows. But by what name are we to call you?" "My name is Cnemon." "From what part of Greece do you come?" "From Athens." "What has been your history?" "Forbear," said Cnemon: "why do you attempt to revive the recollection of my sorrows? let us leave this to the tragedians; my story would be an unnecessary aggravation of your own misfortunes; besides, the rest of the night would not suffice to tell the tale, especially as you must need rest and sleep after all your fatigues."

[Cnemon is prevailed upon to tell his story of the machinations of a wicked stepmother and her scheming housemaid which brought him to disaster. He ends by shedding abundant tears.]

The strangers did the same, apparently moved by the tale of his misfortunes, but really at the memory of their own. Their lamentations would never have ceased, had not sleep, induced by the luxury of their grief, suddenly come upon them and dried their tears. Thus, then, they went to sleep. In the meantime, Thyamis (this was the robber chieftain's name), who had rested quietly during the greater part of the night, was afterwards tormented by wandering visions; and, pondering what could be the meaning of the dream, he lay awake all night, plunged in meditation. It was the hour when the cocks begin to crow, either because a natural instinct warns them of the return of the sun to earth and they are moved to salute the god, or because a feeling of warmth and an eager desire to move and eat inclines them to rouse to work those who live in the same house. At this moment the gods sent Thyamis a vision.

He thought that he was in Memphis, his native country; he entered the temple of Isis, which seemed to be one blaze of lamps; the altars were full of all kinds of victims, and dripping with blood; the vestibule of the temple and its open spaces were filled by a noisy and agitated crowd. After he had entered the sanctuary, the goddess came forward to meet him, and presenting Chariclea to him, said:

"Thyamis, I intrust this maiden to your care; you shall possess her without possessing her; you shall be guilty of a crime, you shall cover the stranger with blood, but she shall not die." This vision sorely troubled him: after turning the words over every way in his mind, in order to discover their meaning, he at last gave up the attempt, and interpreted them in accordance with his own desires. "You shall possess her without possessing her," he interpreted to mean that he should have her as a wife, not as a virgin; by the words "you shall cover her with blood," he understood the wounds inflicted upon her virginity, wounds which would not prove mortal. In this manner he explained the vision, agreeably to the suggestions of his passion.

As soon as it was day, he summoned his chief followers, and ordered them to bring the plunder, which he called by the high-sounding name of "spoils," into the midst; he also sent for Cnemon, with instructions to fetch the prisoners who had been intrusted to his care. While they were being conducted to the chief, they exclaimed, "What fate is reserved for us?" and begged Cnemon to assist them in any way he could. He promised to do so, and bade them be of good cheer, assuring them that the chief of the brigands was not an utter barbarian, but was of a kind and gentle disposition; that he belonged to an illustrious family, and had only adopted his present mode of life from necessity.

When they reached his presence, and the whole band had assembled, Thyamis took his seat upon an eminence in the island, the appointed meeting-place, and ordered Cnemon to translate what he said to the prisoners; for, while he had only an imperfect knowledge of Greek, Cnemon had now learned to speak Egyptian. Thyamis then addressed the meeting as follows: "Comrades, you know what my feelings towards you have always been. You are aware that, being the son of a priest of Memphis, deprived of my right of succession to the sacerdotal functions, of which a younger brother, after my father's death, had robbed me, in violation of the laws, I took refuge amongst you, in order to avenge myself and recover my dignity. You thought me worthy to be your leader; since then, I have lived with you, without ever claiming any special privileges for myself. When there was money to be distributed, I was content with the same share as each of yourselves; when prisoners were sold, I paid what they fetched into the common stock; for I considered it the duty of a good leader to take upon himself the greatest share of fatigue and to be content with an equal share of the spoils. As to the prisoners, I have enrolled amongst your band those who, from their bodily strength, were likely to be useful to us, and sold the weaker. I have never been guilty of violence towards the women; those of noble birth I have released either on payment of ransom, or out of pure compassion for their lot; those of lower rank, who were condemned to slavery by habit rather than the rights of war, I have distributed amongst you as servants. On the present occasion, I ask nothing from you out of all this booty, except this stranger maiden; although I might have claimed her by right, I yet think it better to receive her from you by common consent; for it would be foolish to seem to be acting against the wishes of my friends by appropriating a prisoner by force. However, I do not ask even her from you for nothing; in return, I resign all share in the rest of the booty. The priestly caste despises indiscriminate love; I have made up my mind to wed this maiden, not to satisfy my lust, but in order to propagate my family.

"I will also tell you the reasons which have led me to act thus. In the first place, she appears to me to be well born; this I conjecture from the money found upon her, and also because she is by no means overwhelmed by her misfortunes, but from the first has met them boldly. Next, I am convinced that she is of a good and virtuous disposition; for if, while she surpasses all in beauty, she yet imposes respect upon all who see her by her modest looks, how can we help thinking highly of her? An even still more weighty reason is, that she seems to me to be the priestess of some god, since, even in her misfortune, she considers it an offence against religion to put off her garlands and sacred vestments. Could any union be more fitting than that of a priest and priestess?"

All applauded his words, and wished him a happy marriage, under favourable auspices. Then Thyamis continued: "I thank you, my friends; but we shall now do well to enquire what the maiden thinks about the matter. If I were disposed to make use of the right of authority, my wish alone would be sufficient; for those who can command obedience have no need to ask. But, in the case of lawful marriage, mutual consent is necessary." Then, addressing himself to Chariclea, he said: "What do you think of the proposal that we should marry? Tell me, who are you two, and who are your parents?" Chariclea remained for a long time with her eyes fixed upon the ground, shaking her head from time to time, as if she were collecting her thoughts before answering. When at length she lifted her eyes towards Thyamis, her beauty dazzled him even more than before; for her cheeks, animated by her thoughts, were ruddier than usual, and her kindling eyes were full of vehemence. Then, Cnemon acting as interpreter, she thus addressed Thyamis: "It would be more seemly that my brother Theagenes should answer; for I think that silence becomes a woman, and that it is a man's duty to answer amongst men.

"But, since you have invited me to speak, and have given us in this the first proof of your humanity, showing that you wish to obtain what you have a right to claim by persuasion rather than by force (since everything that has been said concerns myself), I feel compelled to abandon my usual practice and that of my sex, and even in the presence of so large an audience of men, to reply to the question put to me by him who is now my master. Listen, then, to the following account of us:

"We are Ionians: our family is one of the most illustrious in Ephesus. When we had attained to years of discretion, we were summoned by the law to undertake priestly functions; I was consecrated to Artemis, and my brother to Apollo. These functions last a year. When our term was over, we had to set out for Delos on the sacred embassy, to arrange the athletic sports and contests of music, and to lay down our priestly office in accordance with the established custom. For this purpose, a vessel was loaded with gold, silver, garments, and all that was necessary to invest with suitable dignity the public feast and entertainments. We set sail; our parents, already advanced in years, being afraid of the sea and the voyage, remained at home; but a large number of the citizens accompanied us, either on board our vessel, or upon others which they had fitted out themselves. When the voyage was nearly over, a storm suddenly arose; a violent hurricane, accompanied by thunder and lightning, lifted up the waves, and drove the ship out of its course; the pilot, obliged to yield to the fury of the storm, abandoned the helm, and allowed the vessel to drift haphazard. Seven days and seven nights we were borne along by the wind that never ceased, until at last we were cast upon the shore where we were found by you, and where you saw the traces of the great slaughter that had taken place. I must explain how it happened. The sailors conspired against us, while we were celebrating a feast in thanksgiving for our preservation, and resolved to kill us and seize our property.

A terrible struggle ensued, in which all our companions perished, while the sailors themselves slew and were slain: we alone survived the diaster—and would to Heaven we had not!—we alone remain, a miserable remnant. Our only consolation amidst our misfortunes is, that some god has brought us into your hands; and that we, who feared for our lives, have been granted permission to discuss the question of my marriage, which I certainly do not desire to decline. The idea that I, a captive, should be considered worthy of my master's bed, is indeed too great a happiness! And further, that a maiden, consecrated to the service of God, should be united to the son of a priest, who will soon, with Heaven's approval, be a priest himself, this is clearly the work of divine Providence. I only ask you, Thyamis, to grant me one favour: let me first go to the city, or wherever there is a temple or altar dedicated to Apollo, to lay aside my priesthood and deposit there these badges of my office. The best thing would be to wait until you return to Memphis, when you receive the dignity of priesthood; in this manner, our marriage would be more joyful as being associated with victory and celebrated after success. However, I leave it to you to decide whether it shall take place sooner; let me only first perform the sacred rites enjoined by the custom of my country. I know that you will grant my request, since, as you say, you have been devoted to the service of the gods from your infancy, and you are full of respect for everything that concerns them."

With these words she left off speaking, and began to weep.

All those who were present approved, and urged her to do as she proposed, and declared that they were ready to support her. Thyamis also approved, willing and yet unwilling. His passion for Chariclea caused him to look upon the delay of a single hour as an eternity. But, on the other hand, her words, like some siren's song, charmed him and compelled him to assent. Besides, he saw in this some connection with his dream, and believed that the wedding would be celebrated at Memphis. Having distributed the booty, he dismissed the assembly; he himself obtained some of the most valuable articles, a voluntary gift from his comrades.

They were ordered to hold themselves in readiness to proceed to Memphis in ten days' time. He assigned the same tent to the young Greeks as before, and ordered that Cnemon should attend them, no longer as their custodian, but as their friend and companion. He also gave them more luxurious food than he ate himself, and sometimes invited Theagenes to his table, out of regard for his sister. He had resolved to see Chariclea only rarely and at intervals, for fear the sight of her might still more inflame his violent passion and drive him to do something contrary to the agreement that had been entered into. For these reasons Thyamis avoided her presence, thinking that, if he saw her, he would find it impossible to restrain himself.

As soon as the meeting had broken up, and all had dispersed to their several quarters in the marsh, Cnemon went some little distance from the lake, to look for the herb which he had promised Theagenes the day before.

Meanwhile Theagenes, taking advantage of the freedom afforded him, began to weep and sob; he did not address a word to Chariclea, but called upon the gods without ceasing. Thereupon the maiden asked him whether he was only lamenting their common misfortunes, or whether anything fresh had happened. "What fresh misfortune could be worse?" replied Theagenes; "what greater infidelity, what greater violation of vows and promises could there be than that Chariclea should forget me, and consent to another union?" "Hush!" said the maiden; "be not more cruel to me

than my misfortunes; do not, after so many proofs of my
fidelity in the past, suspect me in consequence of words
uttered under stress of circumstances, and adapted to the
necessities of the moment. Otherwise, you will show that
you are changed yourself rather than that you have found
any change in me. I am ready to endure unhappiness; but
no force in the world will ever persuade me to do anything
that virtue forbids. I know that in one thing alone I am
immoderate—my passion for you; but this is lawful and
honourable. I did not yield to you as a lover; I abandoned
myself entire to you from the first, as a husband with
whom I had made a solemn compact; hitherto, I have kept
myself pure from all illegitimate intercourse with you; I
have frequently repelled your advances, waiting for the
opportunity of legitimately consecrating that union to
which we have been pledged from the commencement, and
which has been confirmed by most solemn oaths. Besides,
you could not be so foolish as to think that I should prefer a
barbarian to a Greek, a brigand to one whom I love!"

"What, then, was the meaning of your fine speech?"
asked Theagenes. "Your idea of calling me your brother
was a very wise precaution, which prevented Thyamis
from being jealous of our affection for each other, and
allowed us to associate freely and without fear. I understood that all you said about Ionia and our wanderings in
the neighbourhood of Delos were so many fictions to disguise the truth and to mislead your hearers.

"But, when you showed yourself so ready to agree to the
proposal of Thyamis, definitely promised to marry him,
and even fixed the day, I neither could nor would understand what it meant; rather, I wished that the earth had
opened and swallowed me up before I had lived to see such
a result of my hopes and labours on your behalf."

At these words Chariclea embraced Theagenes, covered him with kisses, and watered his face with her tears. "How delightful to me are your fears on my account! They prove that your love for me is not shaken, in spite of our calamities. Be assured, Theagenes, that had I not made this promise, we should not be conversing together at the present moment. Resistance, as you are aware, only aggravates a violent passion; whereas yielding words, calculated to humour the will, soothe its first outbursts, and blunt the edge of desire by the delights of which they hold out promise in the future. Those who love most fiercely consider a first attempt implies consent, and, thinking that possession will follow, grow calmer, resting on their hopes. This consideration made me yield to Thyamis in words, leaving the future issue to the gods and the Genius who, from the beginning, has taken our love under his protection. An interval of a day or two is often most salutary, and Fortune brings means of safety which no human wisdom can devise. Wherefore I have deferred the present by my inventiveness, putting off the certainties of the present by the uncertainties of the future. Wherefore, my dearest, we must use this fiction as a wrestler's trick and conceal it not only from the rest, but even from Cnemon. For, although he is kindly disposed to us, and is a Greek, he is, like ourselves, a prisoner, and therefore more likely to try and gain his master's favour, should the opportunity occur. Neither the time our acquaintance has lasted nor the ties of kindred race are sufficiently sure pledges of his fidelity to us; wherefore, should he at any time touch upon the truth, you must flatly deny it. For a lie is sometimes permissible, even praiseworthy, when it benefits those who tell it and does no harm to those who hear it."

While Chariclea was thus suggesting to Theagenes the

best course to take, Cnemon entered in great haste, with agitation depicted in his looks. "Oh, Theagenes!" said he, "here is the herb which I promised you; take and apply it to your wounds. But we must be prepared for other wounds, and another massacre such as that you have already witnessed." Theagenes begged him to explain himself more clearly. "It is not the time to tell you now," he answered; "there is reason to fear that words might be anticipated by deeds. But follow me without delay, both you and Chariclea." He then conducted them both to Thyamis, whom they found polishing his helmet and sharpening his spear, and said to him: "Your employment is opportune; gird on your arms and order your comrades to do the like. We are threatened by foes more numerous than we have yet encountered; they are close upon us; I descried them advancing over the top of the hill, and have hastened with all speed to announce their approach. I have also warned all those whom I met to get ready for battle."

At these words, Thyamis started up, and asked where Chariclea was, as if he feared more for her than for himself. When Cnemon showed her trembling at the entrance of the tent, Thyamis whispered in his ear: "Take her into the cave where all our treasures are stored; and when you have taken her down, close the entrance in the usual way, and come back to me with all speed; we must make arrangements for the fight." At the same time he ordered his armour-bearer to bring him a victim, that he might offer sacrifice to the gods of the place, before beginning battle.

Obedient to orders, Cnemon led away Chariclea, who sighed and lamented and kept looking back at Theagenes, and shut her down in the cave. This cave was not the work of nature, like many others that are hollowed out on the surface and in the interior of the earth. The art of the brigands had imitated nature, and had cleverly hollowed it out as a receptacle for their spoils.

It was constructed in the following manner: Its entrance was narrow and dark, made beneath the door of a secret chamber, the threshold of which was another door, which easily shut and opened upon the entrance, and afforded a passage for descent, whenever necessary; within were a number of winding paths, cut at haphazard. These paths or galleries, sometimes separate and winding alone, sometimes purposely connected and intertwined like roots of trees, all converged into an open space at the bottom, which was dimly lighted through an opening in the lower part of the marsh. Here Cnemon made Chariclea descend; he led her by the hand to the inmost recesses of the cave, along the winding passages with which he was familiar, encouraging her in every way he could, and promising to return for her in the evening with Theagenes, whom he said he would not permit to take part in the coming engagement, but would keep him out of the way. Chariclea did not utter a word; she appeared stricken to death, deprived of Theagenes, her life and soul. He left her scarcely breathing and silent, and came up from the cave. Then he shut down the door, shedding tears over her lot and the necessity which compelled him to bury her alive, and to deliver over to darkness and obscurity the most beautiful of human beings. After this, he hastened back to Thyamis, whom he found burning with eagerness for the fray, and splendidly armed, with Theagenes by his side. In order to arouse to frenzy the warlike spirit of his comrades who surrounded him, he stood up in the midst, and thus addressed them:

"Comrades, I know that I need not exhort you at length; you want no encouragement, for you have always looked upon war as the breath of life. Besides, the sudden approach of the enemy cuts short all lengthy discourse. Those who, when the enemy attacks them, do not promptly prepare to repulse them by the same means, show themselves utterly ignorant of their duty. Know, then, that it is not a question of defending your wives and children, which alone in the case of many would be sufficient to rouse their spirits to battle; for these and other like advantages to which we attach less importance, together with those that victory brings, will remain ours if we overcome our foes. But it is a question of our very existence, of our life; no quarter is given, a truce is unknown in wars between pirates; life is the reward of victory, defeat is death. Let us therefore fall upon our hated foes with fury of mind and body."

Having said this, he looked round for his squire, Thermuthis, and called him several times by name. When he did not appear, he burst out into violent threats against him, and hastened to the boats. For the battle had already begun, and he was able to see from a distance the inhabitants of the extremity and approaches of the marsh in the hands of the enemy, who had set fire to the boats and huts of those who had fallen or sought safety in flight. The flames spread to the neighbouring morass, and consumed the reeds which grew there in great abundance; the conflagration shed around a mighty and intolerable blaze, that dazzled the eyes, while the ears were stunned with the sharp crackling and roaring of the flames.

War, in every form and shape, was seen and heard; the inhabitants sustained the combat with all possible courage and vigour; but the enemy, who possessed the advantage of superior numbers and the suddenness of their attack, slaughtered some upon land, and overwhelmed others in the marsh with their boats and huts. In the midst of the tumult, a dull and confused sound rose in the air, as if the engagement were going on both on land and water; the combatants slew and were slain; the waters of the lake were stained with blood, and all were confusedly mingled with fire and water. Thyamis, at this sight and the terrible noise, suddenly remembered the vision, in which he had seen Isis and her temple, resplendent with lamps and full of victims for sacrifice; he saw in it the representation of what he now beheld, and, putting quite a different interpretation upon it from his earlier one, he thought that the words "you shall possess her, and yet shall not possess her" signified that Chariclea would be carried off from him by war, and that the words "you shall slay her and not merely wound her" referred to the sword, and not to the contest of love. He heaped abuse upon the goddess for having deceived him; and, exasperated at the thought that another should possess Chariclea, he bade his comrades halt, and if they were obliged to fight, to carry on a war of ambuscade where they stood, and make secret sallies into the marshes around them, although even thus they would find it difficult to resist the enemy's superior numbers.

He himself, under pretence of going to look for Thermuthis, and offering up prayers to his household gods, gave orders that no one should follow him, and returned, almost beside himself, to his tent. It is in the nature of barbarians not to allow themselves to be turned aside from the object they have in view; when they despair of their own safety, they begin by slaying all those whom they hold most dear, either in the false belief that they will be with them again after death, or that, in so doing, they are delivering them from the violence and insults of the enemy. Thus Thyamis, forgetting all the dangers by which he was threatened, at the very moment when the enemy surrounded him like a net, raging with anger, love, and jealousy, hurried with all speed to the cave, and leaped down, crying out with all his might in the Egyptian language. At the entrance he found a woman who addressed him in Greek; her voice guided him to her person; he seized her hair with his left hand, and plunged his sword into her bosom.

The unhappy woman uttered a piteous groan, and fell lifeless on the ground. Thyamis hastened up, closed the entrance, and flung a few handfuls of earth upon it, saying: "Let this be my wedding present!" He then made his way to the boats, where he found his companions preparing to take to flight, since the enemy could be seen close at hand; at the same time, Thermuthis arrived with a victim for the sacrifice. Thyamis reviled him, told him that he had anticipated him by offering the most beautiful of victims, and got into a boat, accompanied by Thermuthis and a rower, these boats, consisting of a single piece of wood and rudely hollowed out of the trunk of a tree, being unable to hold more than three. Accordingly, Theagenes and Cnemon got into another boat, and the rest did the same. When all had embarked, they retired to a little distance from the island, and at first rowed round it instead of going out into the open sea; soon they even ceased rowing, and drew up their boats in line, ready to meet the attack of the enemy. But, at the mere approach of the latter, as soon as they saw them, the brigands took to flight, frightened at the violence of the waves alone and thrown into confusion by the sound of their war cry. Cnemon and Theagenes also retreated, but not from fear. Thyamis alone, either because he thought it would be disgraceful to flee, or because he could not endure the idea of surviving Chariclea, rushed into the midst of his enemies.

Already he was engaged with them, when some one cried out, "It is Thyamis; do not lose sight of him." Then immediately the boats surrounded and shut him in on all sides. He fought stoutly, wounding some and killing others; but the most astonishing thing was what happened afterwards; in spite of their numbers, not one of the enemy lifted up the sword, or hurled a javelin against him; their only object seemed to be to capture him alive. For a long time Thyamis resisted with all his might; but at last, a body of men rushed upon him, and tore his spear from his hands. He also lost his armour-bearer, who had bravely assisted him, but at length, believing himself mortally wounded, and despairing of his life, flung himself into the lake, swam out of reach, and although with considerable difficulty, safely gained the land, since the enemy did not think it worth while to pursue him; for, as they had already captured Thyamis, they regarded this as a complete victory. The loss of a great number of their comrades was more than compensated by the capture alive of the man who had been chiefly responsible for it. So true is it that all brigands hold money dearer than life itself, and the rights of friendship and kinship are sacrificed to greed alone. It was so in this case; for the victors were the very same who had formerly taken to flight before Thyamis and his comrades at the Hercules mouth of the Nile. Indignant at being deprived of that which was not really theirs, and as furious at the loss of the spoils as if they had been their own property, they gathered together their comrades who had remained at home and called upon the neighbouring villages for assistance, and, offering them an equal share of any spoils that might be taken, put themselves at the head of the expedition.

The following was the reason why they took Thyamis alive. He had a brother named Petosiris living at Memphis, who had by intrigue dispossessed him of the dignity of chief priest, contrary to the custom of the country (for he was the younger brother). This Petosiris, having heard that his elder brother had become the captain of a band of brigands, and being afraid that, if he found an opportunity, he might return to Memphis, or that time might reveal his treachery; and, in addition, seeing that he was suspected of having made away with his brother, who had disappeared, he sent messengers into the villages inhabited by the brigands, offering a large sum of money and a large number of cattle to any who should capture Thyamis alive and bring him to him. The brigands, seduced by these offers, even in the heat of battle did not forget the hope of gain held out to them; and, as soon as Thyamis was recognised, did not hesitate to sacrifice a number of their comrades, in order to take him alive. When they had captured him, they put him in irons and rowed him to land, half of their number being deputed to guard him, while he reproached them bitterly for their apparent humanity and expressed greater indignation at his imprisonment than if it had been death itself. The others, meanwhile, returned to the island, in the hope of finding the treasures and booty of which they were in search, and scoured it thoroughly, leaving no part unexplored. But, finding nothing of all that they had set their hearts upon, with the exception of a few articles of trifling value, which the owners had forgotten to hide in the underground cave, they set fire to the tents. Then, since night was approaching, being afraid to remain longer in the island, lest they should fall into the hands of those who had escaped from the battle, they returned to their comrades.

[For the further adventures of Theagenes and of Chariclea (who of course was not the woman Thyamis had killed) you must read the novel.]

ALEXANDER, THE BRAHMINS,
AND QUEEN CANDACE

BY PSEUDO-CALLISTHENES

The *Life of Alexander of Macedon* is a *vie romancée*, a biographical novel, a compound of fact and fiction. The facts of Alexander's conquering excursion to the east make one of the great true stories of all time. This *Life of Alexander* adorns the frame of old tradition with picturesque inventions, and presents Alexander as the impeccable knightly hero.

The book was written about A.D. 300, perhaps as a development of earlier versions, now lost. The author is unknown. He was once conjectured to be Callisthenes, nephew of Aristotle. The conjecture having been overthrown, the author has only the humiliating title of Pseudo-Callisthenes.

This *Life of Alexander* had an immense vogue throughout the medieval world. Versions in twenty-four languages, from as far away as Malaya, are known. Our own rendering, from *The Life of Alexander of Macedon*, translated by Elizabeth H. Haight, appeared under the imprint of Longmans, Green, and Company in 1955, and is used by permission of David McKay Company, Inc.

[Alexander has reached India on his great journey of conquest.]

Now ALEXANDER made a journey to the Oxydrakes,* not because they were warriors, but because they were gymnosophists,† who had retired to huts and caves. They wrote a letter to him:

"We, the Brachmanes, the gymnosophists, have written to Alexander, a human being. If you come to us to make war, you will gain nothing. For we have nothing which

---

* Oxydrakes: "Sharp-eyed."—Ed.

† Gymnosophists: "naked philosophers"; Brahmin ascetics.—Ed.

you can carry off. But if you wish what we have, there is no need to fight for it. For your occupation is to make war, ours is to study philosophy."

Thus informed, Alexander made a peaceful approach to them and saw that all were half-naked. So he asked: "Do you not occupy tombs?" They said: "This is the place where we stay and ours. . . ." * And turning to another, he said: "Who are the more numerous, the dead or the living?" They replied: "The dead are the more numerous, but do not count those who no longer exist. For those seen are more numerous than those no longer visible." And he inquired of another: "Which is stronger, death or life?" He said: "Life, because the sun when it rises has stronger rays but, when it sets, it is clearly weaker." He said again: "Which is greater, the land, or the sea?" He said: "The land. For the sea is placed upon the land." He asked: "Which of all creatures is more competent?" And he said: "Man." He asked: "Who is there whom we cannot deceive, to whom we always present the truth?" "God, for we cannot deceive the all-seeing."

He said to them: "What do you wish to demand of me?" They said: "Immortality." Alexander said: "This power I do not have. For I am but a mortal." They said: "Why, then, being a mortal, do you enter upon such great wars? Is it that, having seized all treasures, you may carry them away to some other place? You again will leave them to others." And Alexander said to them: "These matters lie on the lap of the gods, that we may be servants of their rule. For the sea is not moved unless a wind blows, and trees are not shaken unless the air stirs, and man is not set in motion except by the will of god. I wish to cease from war,

* The ellipses here and elsewhere in the story are in the original. —Ed.

but the tyranny of my mind does not let me. For if we all were of one mind, the cosmos would be inactive, sea not be filled, earth not be cultivated, marriages not consummated, children not produced. How many in the wars instigated by me had the misfortune of losing their possessions? How many others made fortunes from the possessions of others? Yes, all who seize the possessions of all men give way to others, and nothing belongs permanently to any man."

After this speech, Alexander departed.

[Now Alexander wrote a letter to Aristotle about his experiences]

"King Alexander sends greeting to Aristotle. I must relate our astonishing experiences in the land of India. For when we came to the city of Prasias, which is apparently the capital of India, we found near it a conspicuous promontory by the sea. When I went with a few companions to this cliff, we learned by inquiry that human beings with the forms of women lived there, who subsisted on fish. When I called some of them to me, I found that they spoke a barbarian language. And when I inquired about the region, they pointed out to me an island which we all saw far out at sea, and they said it was the burial place of an ancient king and in it there were many dedications of gold. The barbarians vanished leaving behind their small boats, twelve in all. Then Pheidon, my closest friend, and Hephaistion, and Krateros and my other companions would not allow me to go across, for Pheidon said: 'Permit me to make the voyage before you in order that, if there is any danger there, I rather than you will run the risk of disaster. If there is not, I will later send back the skiff. For if I, Pheidon, perish, you will find other friends. But if you, Alexander, perish, the whole world has suffered loss.' So, persuaded by them, I agreed to this plan. After they landed on the so-called island and an hour passed, suddenly <it proved to be no island, but a> * monster which plunged into the sea. We shouted and it disappeared, but some of my companions met a wretched death, among them my best friend. I was enraged, but, though I hunted for the barbarians, I did not find them. We stayed eight days on the rock and on the seventh we saw the beast and it had tusks. That was long enough to stay, so we went back to the city of Prasias.

"We came upon many remarkable things which I must tell you about. For I saw all sorts of wild beasts and marvellous natural phenomena, many kinds of serpents, and, most wonderful of all, an eclipse of the sun and moon. The winter was severe. We conquered Darius, king of the Persians, and his army and after having subdued the whole region we proceeded on our way, and saw beautiful objects. There was gold. There were mixing bowls decorated with precious stones. One crater held one and a half cotulae,† another eight, and there were many other marvellous objects.

"We started our trek from the Caspian Gates and from there went on. Soon the trumpeter announced it was the tenth hour of the day. For at sunrise the trumpet sounded and we marched four hours. The soldiers were equipped in this manner: the body of each was protected by shoes, leggings, leather coverings for thighs, cuirasses. For the natives had informed us that there were dangerous snakes on these roads. So I issued orders that everyone should be fitted out in this way.

"After we had travelled twelve days, we came to a city which was in the middle of the river. Reeds grew about the

* The angle brackets are the translator's.—Ed.
† Cotula: about half a pint.—Ed.

city, thirty cubits * long, and surrounded it and the city was built out of them. It did not lie on the ground, but floated on the reeds I have mentioned. I gave orders to pitch camp here. So, after making camp, in the third hour of the day we went to the river and found the water more bitter than hellebore. When some men wished to swim into the city, hippopotami appeared and seized them. The only thing for us to do was to leave the region. So the trumpet sounded and we marched from the sixth hour until the eleventh and we were so distressed by lack of water that I saw soldiers using their own urine. By good fortune we came to a certain district where there was a fertile swamp with trees and assembling there we found water so sweet that it tasted like honey. So while we were in a very happy mood, we saw on the hill a stele with an inscription. These were the words carved on it: 'Sesonchosis, ruler of the world, made this watering-place for those who sail the Red Sea.'

"Then I gave order to make a camp and prepare for a rest and kindle a fire. There was a bright moon and stars. About the third hour of the night, wild beasts from the whole forest near the camp I have mentioned came to the watering-place. There were scorpions, a cubit long, sand burrowers, some white, some flame colored. And we were not ⟨successful⟩ in fighting them; indeed, some men perished; you heard loud cries and groans of those who succumbed. Then four-footed beasts began to arrive at the watering-place. There were lions larger than our bulls and rhinoceroses. They all came out of the reeds in the wood. There were wild boars larger than the lions with tusks a cubit long, lynxes, leopards, tigers, scorpions, elephants and wild cattle and bull elephants, and men with six hands and crooked legs, and dogbirds and other monsters.

* Cubit: one and a half feet.—Ed.

We had to fight them at once and we warded them off with out axes . . . and wolves came from the sand, some of them ten cubits, others of eight. And from the wood came crocodiles which destroyed our baggage. There were bats bigger than pigeons, bats with teeth. And near the swamp sat crows which we hunted. It was a marvellous sight. . . .

"After we had organized everything, we came to the natural road which leads to the Prasiakan land. And when I was prepared to start on, about the sixth hour, there occurred a strange phenomenon in the sky. It was the third day of the month Dios. First suddenly there was a high wind so that the tents were hurled down and those of us who were standing fell to the ground. . . .

"Now after thirty days, as the road was passable, we made our way onward and on the fifth day we took the city of Prasias with Poros and his men. It was full of treasures, which I have described. When this happened and I was organizing everything properly, the Indians assembled in numbers and addressed me: 'King Alexander, you will take cities and kingdoms and mountains and tribes which no king among the living ever approached before.' . . . And some learned men came and said: 'King, we have a marvel to show you worthy of your attention. For we will show you inanimate objects which talk like men.' And they led us to a certain park, where in the center were the Sun and the Moon. . . . And there was a guard for the precinct of the Sun and the Moon. Here stood two trees which I have already mentioned. They were about the size of cypresses. . . . And in a circle were the trees mentioned, very like the fragrant chestnut trees in Egypt and their fruit was similar. They said that one was male and produced males; the other female and produced females; and one was called the Sun, the other the Moon. So the natives told the story in their peculiar language. The trees had been hung with various hides of wild beasts, the male with hides of males, the female with females. And there was no iron near, nor bronze, nor tin, nor clay for the potter's art. And when I asked what the hides seemed to be, they said hides of lions and leopards; and it was not possible to have a burial unless the priest of the Sun and the Moon presided. And the hides of the wild beasts were used for the cerements.

"Now I sought to learn the significance of the trees. They said: 'When it is early and the sun rises, the speech of the tree is heard; also when the sun is in mid heaven, and when it is near setting,—the third time. And the same is true of the moon.' And men who appeared to be priests came and said: 'Enter with a pure heart and prostrate yourself.' I took in my friends Parmenion, Krateros, ⟨Philip⟩, Iollas, Machetes, Thrasyleon, ⟨Machaon⟩, Theodektes, Diiphilos, Neokles, ten in all. The priest said: 'King, it is not fitting that metal should enter the precinct.' So I ordered my friends to leave their swords outside. From my forces, three hundred men came without weapons. And I ordered all my army to stand guard in a circle about the spot. And I selected from the Indians with me some to act as interpreters. I invoked Olympian Ammon, Athena, giver of victory, all the gods.

"At the rising of the sun, an Indian voice issued from the tree, which was interpreted by the Indians with me. And from fear they did not wish to share with me their interpretation. I became anxious and upbraided them, and the Indians then said: 'Soon you must die by the hands of your friends.' Now I and those standing by me were stricken by the revelation, and I wished again to secure an oracle from the Moon at its rising in the evening. So, having foreseen the future, I entered and asked if I should again embrace my mother Olympias and the friends dear to me. And again, while my friends stood near me, at the rising of the Moon the tree gave the same oracle in the Greek language: 'King Alexander, you must die in Babylon. By your own people will you be killed and you will not be able to return to your mother Olympias.'

"Now I and my friends were greatly amazed and I wished to hang beautiful garlands upon the gods. But the priest said: 'It is not permitted to do this. But if force is used, do what you wish. For there is no law recorded for a king.'

"Then, as I lay very sorrowful and depressed, Parmenion and Philip urged me to get some sleep. But I could not. I got up wide awake and at sunrise with my ten friends, the priest, and the Indians I went again to the shrine and, issuing special orders, I entered the precinct with the priest and, stretching out my hand to the tree, I made inquiry in these words: 'If the years of my life have been fulfilled, I wish to learn from you this: shall I be carried back to Macedonia and comfort my mother and my wife, and then depart?' Then the sun rose and cast its light on the top of the tree and a voice was heard, saying: 'The years of your life have been fulfilled, and you will not be carried back to your mother Olympias, but you will die in Babylon. And after a little time, your mother and your wife will meet a bitter end at the hands of their people and your brothers too at the hands of your companions. Make no more inquiries about these matters, for you will not hear more about what you ask.'

"So I departed from there about the first hour. . . . From the Prasiakan land I proceeded to Persia, and hastened to the palace of Semiramis. I considered it imperative to write these matters to you. Farewell."

After writing this letter to Aristotle, Alexander led his forces to the kingdom of Semiramis. For he was exceedingly eager to see it, since it was very famous throughout the whole country and Hellas. . . . And a woman ruled the city, a very beautiful woman, who was middle-aged, a widow, mother of three sons. Her name was Candace. She was a descendant of the Queen Semiramis. To her Alexander sent this letter:

"King Alexander sends greetings to Queen Candace in Meroe and to the rulers under her. When I was in Egypt, I heard ⟨of you⟩ from the priests there and saw your graves and dwellings, which showed that you had ruled Egypt. ⟨I heard⟩ that Ammon made an expedition with you, and after a short time on Ammon's advice you returned to your own city. This is the point of my sending a letter to you. Bring the shrine and statue of Ammon to the frontier that we may make a sacrifice to it. But if you do not wish to come with it, let us meet soon in Meroe and have a conference. Let me know your wish there."

Candace wrote back to him:

"Queen Candace of Meroe and the rulers under her send greetings to King Alexander. Of old, Ammon gave an oracle that we should make an expedition into Egypt, and now he has advised that he should not be moved ⟨by me⟩ and that no one should come to me, and that we should repulse those who come to us and treat them as enemies. Do not make a mistake about our race. We are whiter in skin and more shining in soul than the whitest with you. We possess eighty phalanxes ready to attack those entering our land. You will do well by honoring divine Ammon. My ambassadors carry to you one hundred solid bricks of gold, five hundred young Ethiopians, two hundred parrots, two hundred sphinxes, and for our god Ammon, who presides over the boundaries of Egypt, a crown of emeralds and whole pearls, ten chains with seals attached, . . . eighty ivory caskets. Also our gifts include different kinds of wild beasts: three hundred and fifty elephants, three hundred leopards, eighty rhinoceroses, four thousand panthers, six man-eating dogs in cages, three hundred huge bulls, six elephants' tusks, three hundred hides of leopards, fifteen hundred ebony rods. Send at once those whom you wish to receive these gifts, and write us when you have conquered the whole world."

Alexander on receiving and reading the letter sent Kleomenes, overseer of Egypt, to receive the gifts. He himself set off on the journey to her. Now Candace, after hearing about Alexander, how many cities he had stormed and how many kings he had mastered, spoke to one of her artists and ordered him to travel as if for a conference with him and surreptitiously to paint a portrait of Alexander and on his return to give it to her. On receiving it, she put it in a secret hiding place.

Now something else happened. The son of Candace, called Candaules, with a few horsemen, rode down to the camp of Alexander. The guards there took him and presented him to Ptolemy Soter who was at the right of the king's tent, for Alexander was asleep. Ptolemy asked him: "Who are you?" He said: "The son of Candace the queen." The other asked: "Why then are you here?" He replied: "I was travelling with my wife and a small escort to celebrate the annual mysteries among the Amazons. The ruler of the Bebrycians, on seeing that I had a wife with me, came with a great army, carried her off, and killed most of my soldiers. So I turned back to assemble a larger force and destroy the Bebrycians." On hearing all this, Ptolemy arose and approaching Alexander awoke him and told him what he had heard. Alexander, on hearing the news, was at once aroused, and taking up his diadem he crowned Ptolemy and threw his cloak about him and said: "Advance as though you were Alexander and say: 'Call Antigonos, my companion in arms.' And when I come, tell me what you said for me and say: 'What shall we decide about the man? Give me your advice.'"

Ptolemy went out. The soldiers on seeing him were full of conjectures as to what the impulsive Alexander was again planning. Candaules, on seeing the man in the royal dress, feared that he would order his execution. For he supposed he was Alexander. But Ptolemy said: "Let some one summon Antigonos, my companion in arms." Alexander came. Ptolemy said: "Antigonos, this is Candaules, son of Candace the queen. His wife was stolen from him by the ruler of the Bebrycians. What do you advise me to do?" And he said: "Alexander, I advise you to arm your men and make war on the Bebrycians, that we may rescue this man's wife and return her to him for the honor of his mother." Candaules was delighted on hearing these words. Ptolemy then said: "If you wish this, Antigonos, also do it. As my companion in arms, order the expedition to be prepared."

So they made ready for the expedition on the orders of Ptolemy. And Alexander reached the place by a forced march in one day. And Antigonos said: "Alexander, let us not be seen by the Bebrycians in daylight lest the ruler, somehow getting information, shall kill the wife of this man before the battle. And what sort of glory will we have in victory if Candaules loses his wife? So let us enter the city by night and open the houses, and the populace itself will give back the woman." When Antigonos proposed this, Candaules embraced him and said: "How wise you are,

Antigonos! Would that you were Alexander and not the companion in arms of Alexander!" And so in the night they came to the city and, as the inhabitants were asleep, they started fires in the suburbs. And when the men were awakened and inquired what the cause of the fire was, Alexander ordered the soldier to shout: "Candaules the king is here with a great army and gives you this command: 'Give back my wife before I set fire to the whole city.'" So all, taken by surprise and being against their ruler, opened the palace, found the woman in bed with the ruler, took her away, gave her back to Candaules, and killed the tyrant.

Then Candaules, full of gratitude for the plan and the wisdom of Alexander, embracing him said: "Antigonos, entrust yourself to me and come to my mother that I may give you royal gifts." And Alexander joyfully replied: "Ask the king for me. For I desire also to see the city." And Alexander gave the nod to Ptolemy to send him as his messenger. So Ptolemy said to Candaules: "I wish to salute your mother in a letter. So take Antigonos with you as my messenger and send him back again safely just as I restore both yourself and your wife to safety." And he said: "King, I take this man with me as if he were Alexander himself. And I will send him back to you with royal gifts."

So setting out, he took a suitable escort and the animals and wagons for the journey. And as he travelled, he was amazed at the mountains of various colors, gleaming with crystals, reaching up to the clouds of heaven, and the lofty trees heavy with fruit, not like those of the Greeks, but peculiar marvels. For there were apple trees laden with golden fruit like the citrus fruits of the Greeks, and bunches of grapes that one hand could not hold, and pomegranates the size of chestnuts, larger than ripe ones. Quantities of snakes were killed around the trees and lizards larger than rats and apes as large as the bears in Greece, and many other creatures, thousands, of many colors and strange shapes. There were some holy places and caves with entrances. Candaules said: "Antigonos, these are called the homes of the gods and often in these caves gods reclining on couches are seen by the king when he invokes them. So, if you wish, take a libation and make a sacrifice in these regions and they will appear to you." So spoke Candaules. And they continued their journey and came to the palace, and Candaules' brothers and his mother met them. And as they were about to embrace him, Candaules said: "You are not to embrace me before you welcome the savior of my life and the benefactor of my wife, Antigonos, messenger of King Alexander." And they said: "What protection did he give you?" Then he related to them the story of the abduction of his wife by the Bebrycians and the aid ⟨given him⟩. So his brothers and his mother welcomed Alexander. A splendid and royal banquet was given.

On the next day, Candace appeared wearing her crown. She was a large woman with something divine in her appearance so that Alexander seemed to behold his own mother, Olympias. He saw the palace with its gleaming gold roof and stone walls, beds with covers of silk interwoven with gold, couches with supports of onyx and beryl, the frames fitted with leather strips fastened together, and tables with ivory nails . . . so many that they could not be counted. There were scythe-bearing chariots carved of purple stone with the charioteers and horses so that they seemed ready for a race, and elephants chiselled from the same stone, trampling on the enemies, or whirling up their opponents with their trunks. There were complete ships with their sails, carved from one small stone. There were statues of barbarian gods, which terrified those who saw them because of their murderous aspect. Their shrines rose as high as heaven, were as tall as plane trees or cypresses. There was a flowing river, bubbling with golden foam, another kind of Pactolus. There were rows of pepper trees, hung with ripe fruit.

On seeing these, Alexander was filled with amazement. He was the guest of the brothers of Candaules. And Candaules called his mother and asked her to give the messenger gifts worthy of his intelligence and to send him back. At once Candace took Antigonos by the hand and showed him a bed-room gleaming with shining stone so that the sun appeared to rise inside the marble. And in it were three couches of perfect woods which are imperishable and cannot be destroyed by fire. And the house had been built not with a foundation fixed upon the earth, but supported by four huge square wooden ⟨pillars⟩, and was moved on wheels by twenty elephants. And wherever the king went to make war on a city, he lived in this. And Alexander said to Queen Candace: "All these things ⟨would⟩ demand admiration, if they were among the Greeks and not with you, because they have great mountains of varied colors." Candace was enraged and said: "You have spoken the truth, Alexander." He, struck dumb by his name, turned away. But she said: "Why do you turn away, when addressed as Alexander?" And he said: "Lady, I am called Antigonos, messenger of Alexander."—"Even if you are called Antigonos, with me you are King Alexander. At once I will prove it to you." And, taking him by the hand, she led him to her bed-room and said: "Do you recognize your portrait? Why do you tremble? Why are you troubled? You, the sacker of Persis, the conqueror of the Indians, the man who threw down the trophies of the Medes and Parthians, now without wars or army are in the power of Queen

Candace. So learn, Alexander, that, if any man thinks he is supreme in wisdom above all men, another mortal will display greater wisdom than his." Alexander raged and gnashed his teeth. Candace said: "Why rage? Why gnash your teeth? What can you do?" . . . And he said: "If I had my sword, I would first kill you in order never to be subject to you, and then myself, because I betrayed myself." She answered: "This is a noble and royal speech. But start no contest, Alexander. For as you saved my son and his wife from the Bebrycians, I too will take care that among the barbarians you are not Alexander. For if they know that you are Alexander, they will straightway kill you because it was you who killed Poros. For the wife of my youngest son is the daughter of Poros. So be called Antigonos, for I will guard your secret."

When she finished speaking, she went out with him and said: "My son, Candaules, and Marpessa, my daughter, if you had not found opportunely the army of Alexander, I should not have received you back and you would not have found your wife, so let us be worthy of the messenger of Alexander and give him gifts." Her second son, Karagos, said: "I approve, mother. Alexander saved my brother and his wife. Let us give what you wish." Then her third son spoke: "Mother, desist. My wife is grieved. Her father was killed by Alexander. So she wishes that Alexander should know sorrow, and that having his messenger, this Antigonos, in her power, she should kill him." Candace said: "What good will it do you, son, if you kill this man in this way? It is nothing to Alexander if you kill him thus." Then Candaules said: "But this man saved me and my wife and I must send him back safe to Alexander." He replied: "Then let us fight a duel over him." Candaules answered: "I do not wish that. But if it is your will, you will find me ready." Then Candace was in anguish for fear her sons would fight a duel and, getting Alexander by himself, she said: "Since you are resourceful on every occasion, can you not by thinking find a solution so that my sons will not fight over you?" Alexander said: "Karagos and Candaules, if you kill me in this way, Alexander is not disturbed. For messengers do not affect his honor in war. So if you kill me thus, Alexander has other messengers, many of them. If you wish through me to take your enemy Alexander captive, promise to give me a certain share of the gifts on this condition that I stay with you and so make Alexander arrive, on the ground that you wish to present to him in person the gifts which you have prepared." The brothers agreed. And Candace, marvelling at the cleverness of Alexander, said to him in private: "Alexander, would that you too were my son and that through you I were ruling all the nations! For you have taken the cities not by war, but by great strategy." So he was pleased on being saved by them, and Candace kept his secret.

After a few days, when he departed, Candace presented him with royal gifts: a crown of adamant worth many talents and a breastplate rich in onyx and green jewels and a cloak shining like the stars, all purple, shot with gold, and sent him away with his gifts and her own soldiers.

II
THE ROMANS

THE TRAGEDY OF DIDO
AND AENEAS
BY VIRGIL

Publius Vergilius Maro was born near Mantua, in northern Italy, in 70 B.C. After writing his *Eclogues* and *Georgics* he embarked on his great epic poem, the *Aeneid*. With this he intended to create a Latin rival to the Greek epics, and to celebrate Roman supremacy in literature as in conquest and world rule. After working for eleven years on his *Aeneid*, Virgil died in 19 B.C.

The *Aeneid* is of course one of the world's great poems, and it is perhaps indecent to silence its music by rendering it in prose. But perhaps the story quality of the original is emphasized by a literal translation, without the artifice imposed by English metre and rhyme. The translation, of Book I, lines 494–756, and of the whole of Book IV, is by Morris Bishop.

[Long before the present action, Queen Dido of Tyre and Sidon, in Phoenicia, had led her people to find a new home on the African coast, and had established the proud Punic kingdom in Carthage, close to the present Tunis. Now Aeneas, son of Venus and the mortal Anchises, and the survivors of the fall of Troy have fled westward and have been shipwrecked on the Carthaginian coast. Aeneas and faithful Achates have lost touch with the others. Venus has provided the two with a cloud of invisibility. Thus they visit Dido's palace.]

A ENEAS WAS gazing, transfixed, at the frescoes of the Trojan War ornamenting Dido's palace. Then the queen, beautiful of face and figure, appeared, approaching the temple, in the midst of a throng of handsome youths. As Diana herself leads the dance on the banks of the Eurotas or on the Cynthian hills, stepping daintily, quiver on shoulder, in a cluster of a thousand Oreads, queening over them all—so was Dido, smiling upon her suite and bearing light-heartedly the responsibilities of her kingdom in the making. Surrounded by her soldiers, she took her seat on a high throne under the temple porch, and there she laid down judgments and laws for men, invoking abstract justice or throwing dice in knotty cases.

Then suddenly Aeneas perceived a group advancing: Antheus, Sergestus, brave Cloanthus, and other Trojans. The black storm had scattered their ships and cast them here and there on the shore. Aeneas and Achates were dumbstruck at the sight, and filled with joy—and foreboding. They longed to embrace their friends, but were restrained by apprehension. They kept hidden, wrapped in their sheltering cloud. They pondered on the fate of their companions, wondering where they had left their ships, why these delegates from several vessels were coming to beg a favor, filling the temple with their clamor.

The castaways were granted permission to speak. Thus began the noble Ilioneus in measured tones: "O Queen, to whom Jupiter granted the right to found a new realm and to bring proud peoples under the rule of justice, we luckless Trojans, driven by the winds over many seas, make to you our prayer. Forbid your people to burn our stranded ships; spare our god-fearing band; look kindly on our unhappy lot. We do not come to ravage your Libyan homeland, or to carry loot down to our ships. No such intention dwells in our minds, nor is such impudence the quality of broken men. There is a land which the Greeks call Hesperia, an ancient civilization, mighty in arms, rich of soil. The Oenotrians settled it; and now, it is said, their descendants have named it Italia, after their chief. Thither we took our course. Then suddenly stormy Orion rose from the waves, drove us onto hidden shoals, and with his fierce winds and mighty waves tossed us among beetling rocks. Thus only a handful of us have reached your coasts.

"What sort of men are your subjects? What barbarous polity justifies their behavior? They forbid us refuge on their shores; they threaten war, they warn us off from the least foothold. If your people despise the human race and the arms of mortal men, at least expect that the gods will remember your good deeds and bad.

"Our king was Aeneas, unsurpassed in justice, in greatness of spirit, in the arts of war. If the Fates have preserved him, if he still breathes our common air, if he has not descended to the cruel dark, we have nothing to fear, nor need you regret any aid you may give us. We can still find in Sicilian cities refuge, and military stores, and a friend, noble Acestes of Trojan stock. We beg your permission to haul up our storm-battered vessels and cut ship-timbers and shafts for oars in your woods, that we may joyfully continue on our way to Italy and Latium—if it be granted to us to recover our comrades and our king. But if that boon is denied us, if the Libyan sea possesses you, Father Aeneas, and if we must renounce hope in your son Ascanius, we may at least return to welcoming Sicily and accept Acestes as our king."

Thus spoke Ilioneus, and all the Trojans together shouted their approval.

Then Dido, dropping her eyes, spoke briefly. "Don't be afraid, Trojans; stop worrying. Harsh circumstance and the newness of my country force me to plan ahead, to look on all sides to our security. Who could be ignorant of Aeneas and his followers, of Troy city and its mighty men and the devastation of its great war? Not so unenlightened are our Punic minds, not so far from this Tyrian city does the sun yoke his steeds. Whether you head for great Italy, Saturn's favorite country, or for King Acestes in his Sicilian realm, I shall send you safe with an escort and with ample supplies. Or do you wish to settle here within my bounds and share my authority? The city I am building is yours. Haul your ships ashore. Let there be no distinction between Trojan and Tyrian. I wish only that your great king Aeneas could appear, driven by the same blast! Indeed, I shall send men to scour the beaches and search to the limits of Libya, if by chance he has been cast into our wilds or our settlements."

Aeneas and mighty Achates were deeply stirred by these words. They had been longing for some time to break forth from their enveloping cloud. Achates demanded of Aeneas: "Goddess-born, what are you thinking now? You see that all is safe, that our fleet and our fellows are rescued. Just one, Orontes, is missing; we saw him drowned. Everything else is as your mother foretold." Hardly had he spoken when suddenly the cloak of cloud parted and was dissipated in air. Aeneas stood forth shining in the bright light, with the face and build of a god—for his mother, goddess of beauty, had herself adorned him with rippling hair and the ruddy sheen of youth, and had put a joyful sparkle in his eyes, just as the artist's hand gives luster to ivory, or sets silver or Parian marble in yellow gold.

Then, as all stood amazed, he addressed the queen: "Here am I whom you seek, Aeneas the Trojan, saved from the Libyan waves. O Queen, you who alone have pitied us, the survivors of Troy, battered by all the calamities of land and sea, destitute of all, you welcome us to your city and homeland. It is not in our power to thank you fittingly, nor in the power of any remnants of the Trojans, scattered throughout the world. May the gods properly reward you, if any divinities have regard for the good, and may your own consciousness of right action repay you, if any justice exists. What happy age fathered you? What noble forbears produced such an offspring? As long as rivers flow into the sea, as long as cloud-shadows run down the mountain-side, as long as heaven feeds its flock of stars, so long, however far I wander, will your honor, your name, your glory remain in remembrance."

So he spoke, and clasped Ilioneus with his right hand, Serestus with his left. Then he took the hands of sturdy Gyas, sturdy Cleanthus, and the rest. Sidonian Dido, at first astonished by his appearance, and then by the magnitude of his misfortunes, thus replied: "Goddess-born, what evil fate pursues you through danger and disaster? What power brings you to these savage shores? Are you then that Aeneas whom kindly Venus bore to Trojan Anchises by the waters of Simois? But indeed I remember when Teucer, expelled from his country, came to Sidon, seeking a new kingdom with the aid of Belus, my father. Belus then was sacking rich Cyprus and held it under his sway. Since then I have heard of Troy's downfall, of the Pelasgian kings, and I have known your own name. Your very enemy, Teucer, extolled the Trojans with highest praise, and would have it that he came of the ancient stock of the Teucrians. And so, brave youths, welcome to our habitations. My own fate, not unlike yours, has brought me through many trials to find haven at last in this land. Acquainted with misfortune, I have learned to succor the distressed."

Thus she hinted of her past. And immediately she led Aeneas into her royal palace, and proclaimed a sacrifice in the temples of the gods. She took care to send twenty bulls to the comrades on the seashore, a hundred bristling pigs, a hundred lambs with their ewes, gifts for the day's celebration.

Now the palace interior is furbished with royal splendor, a banquet set up in the midst. Embroidered coverlets of royal purple cushion the couches, the tables are set with massive silver, embossed with golden figures portraying the great deeds of Dido's ancestors, illustrating long tales of ancient heroes from the beginning of her race.

Now Aeneas, whose love for his son would brook no delay, sent Achates on the run to his ships, to report the news to Ascanius and fetch him back to the city's walls. The two were commanded to bring back gifts, salvaged from Troy's ruins, a robe with gold-inwrought figures and a veil with a yellow acanthus border. These were the finery of Greek Helen; she had brought them from Mycenae when she had fled to Pergamum and her unlawful mating. They were the miraculous gifts of her mother, Leda. There was also a scepter, once borne by Ilione, eldest of Priam's daughters, and a necklace with pearl pendants, and a coronet with a double circlet of jewels and gold.

Achates took his orders and hurried to the ships.

Meanwhile the Cytherean goddess was meditating a new trick, whereby Cupid, changed in face and feature, might come in place of sweet Ascanius, and kindle the queen to frenzy and make her veins run with fire. In truth Venus feared this house of treachery and the double-tongued Tyrians. Juno's vindictiveness irritated her; her concern increased with the gathering dark. So she spoke to winged Amor in these words: "My son, my strength, my only power, you who scorn the Titan-killing shafts of Father Jupiter, I appeal to you, and as suppliant I entreat your divinity. Well you know how your half-brother Aeneas has been storm-tossed and cast on many a shore through the hatred of unjust Juno. You have often sympathized with my grief. Now Phoenician Dido possesses him and detains him with her blandishments, and I fear the outcome of such hospitality in Juno's country. The goddess will not hold her hand in such a crisis. And so I plan to take the queen by

craft, to inflame her heart before some power may inter-
vene to change her; I would keep her fast bound to me
through a great love for Aeneas. I will tell you how you
can do this. The princely lad, my own darling, is preparing,
at his father's summons, to go to the Sidonian city, carrying gifts saved from the fire and flood of Troy. But I shall
plunge Ascanius in sleep and hide him on the Cytherean
mountains or in my holy temple above Idalia, so that he
may learn nothing of my schemes, and not blunder into the
middle of them. Now do you, my dear, take on his likeness
in your sly way for not more than a night; assume the boy's
well-known face, so that when Dido joyfully takes you on
her lap at the royal table, while the wine flows free, while
she hugs and kisses you sweetly, you may kindle in her a
secret flame and plant your poison deep."

Cupid accepted the instructions of his dear mother, laid
aside his wings, and delightedly imitated the step of Ascanius. But Venus drenched the limbs of the real Ascanius in
gentle sleep, and, divinely fondling him, bore him to the
high groves of Idalia; and there on a bed of sweet marjoram
he is cradled in flowers and caressed by soothing shade.

Now docilely Cupid has set forth, with Achates for
conductor, and gayly has borne the royal gifts to the Tyrians. When he arrives, the queen has already reclined on a
golden couch, under regal hangings. Now Father Aeneas
and the young Trojans assemble and dispose themselves on
the purple-covered couches. Servants pour water for their
hands, serve bread from baskets, and bring neatly hemmed
napkins. In the pantry fifty kitchenmaids lay out the dishes
in long rows and feed the hearth-fires. A hundred wait-
resses, a hundred waiters, all of the same age, stand ready
to load the tables with food and set out the cups. A throng
of Tyrians crowd the festive halls, bidden to recline on the
embroidered couches. They gape at Aeneas' gifts, they

gape at the false Ascanius, at the young god's glowing cheeks; they wonder at his words, aptly counterfeited, at the robe and veil with its yellow acanthus design. And Dido most of all, the unfortunate doomed queen, cannot satisfy her longing. She fastens her burning glance on the boy; he moves her no less than the costly presents. And Cupid, after warmly embracing Aeneas, stilling the emotion in his supposititious father's bosom, turns to the queen. Poor Dido, all unwitting, devours him with her eyes, brushes him with her bosom, takes him fondly on her knees. The god plays up to the wretched woman. Cupid, faithful to his mother's instructions, begins to erase from Dido's mind recollection of her lost husband Sychaeus and attempts to awaken her long-slumbering soul, her dormant heart, to a living love.

When first came a lull in the feasting and when the tables had been removed the servants brought out the great wine-jugs and wreathed them with garlands. Clamor rose to the roofs, many voices resounded through the wide hall. Blazing chandeliers hung from the gold-fretted ceiling; torches banished the dark with their flame. Then the queen called for her gold cup heavy with jewels, from which ancient Belus and all his line had drunk. Now silence was imposed throughout the hall; and Dido proclaimed: "O Jupiter—for they say that thou dost appoint the laws of hospitality—may it be thy will to bless this day to the Tyrians and to the refugees of Troy; and may our children long remember it! May Bacchus, giver of gladness, attend, and good Juno too! And do you, Tyrians, honor the assembly with a friendly spirit!"

She spoke; and poured upon the table a libation of wine; and afterwards she was the first to touch the cup with her lips. Then she passed it challengingly to the Carthaginian Bitias. He briskly drained the brimming golden cup, and the other chiefs followed suit. Long-haired Iopas, pupil of Atlas himself, made the hall ring with the chords of his golden zither. He sang of the wandering moon and the labors of the sun, of the origin of men and animals, of the source of rain and lightning, of Arcturus and the rainy Hyades and the Great and Little Bear, and why the winter suns hasten so to plunge in the western ocean, and what makes the long wintry nights linger. The Tyrians redoubled their applause, and the Trojans were not far behind them.

Meanwhile luckless Dido chattered away to prolong the evening, and drank her fill of love. She asked many a question about Priam, about Hector. She would learn what weapons Memnon, son of Aurora, bore, what was the race of Diomedes' horses, what was the stature of Achilles. "Come, dear guest," she said to Aeneas, "tell us from the beginning the story of the Greeks' trickeries, of the Trojans' downfall, of your own wanderings; for this is now the seventh summer of your roving over the world's land and waters."

[Aeneas tells the long story of the fall of Troy and the flight of the survivors. His narrative occupies the whole of Books II and III. Book IV begins.]

Queen Dido, with the pangs of love-longing in her heart, cherishes her wound. She burns with a hidden fire. She can think only of the valor of Aeneas, the glory of his stock. His face, his words, are imprinted in her breast; nor can she, by taking thought, appease her inward tumult. And when the first dawn, Phoebus' lamp in hand, brought a glimmer of light and scattered the dewy dark, she spoke wildly to her sympathetic sister: "Dear Anna, what dreams make me quake with fear! What is this guest who has made himself at home with us? How nobly he bears himself!

How broad that chest, battered in many an encounter! I think, surely, that what they say is true—he is of divine origin. He shows no fear—the mark of petty souls. Oh dear, how he has been persecuted by fate! What everlasting wars he told us of! If it weren't for my fixed and immovable purpose never to submit to the marriage bond, since my first experience was unhappily ended by death, if I were not revolted by the marriage ceremony, I could have yielded to him alone in forbidden union. Anna, I'll admit to you, since the death of my poor Sychaeus—since he was murdered by his brother-in-law—Aeneas alone has roused my senses and made my intention waver. I recognize the marks of old passion. But rather would I see earth yawn for me, down to its core, or see the Almighty smite me with a fatal thunderbolt, to dwell in dark night among the pallid shades of Erebus, than would I violate the precepts of honor and decency. My first husband took away with him all my love; let him preserve and treasure it in the tomb."

So she spoke, and drenched her bosom with welling tears. Anna rejoined: "Sister, dearer to me than the light of life, will you pine away, lonely and sad, all your youth long? Will you not know the gifts of Venus, the delights of motherhood? Do you think that buried ashes or dim ghosts still care? Granted that no suitors so far have chased your grief, whether in Libya or before that in Tyre. You rejected Iarbas and the other mighty men of this stormy African land; but will you still struggle against a welcome love? Do you give no thought to this country where you have settled? On one side we have Getulian cities of a people unconquerable in war, bordered by the bridleless Numidians and the indomitable Syrtes; on the other side the waterless desert and the savage nomad Barcaeans. And how about the looming war with Tyre and the threats of your brother? It was evidently with divine favor and the consent of Juno that the Trojan ships made their way here with fair winds. Imagine the city, the kingdom, that you could build with a spouse like Aeneas! With the aid of Trojan arms, to what glory would Carthage attain! Then implore the gods' favor, make due sacrifices, offer cordial welcome, invent pretexts for delay, while winter and watery Orion roughen the seas, the ships lie shattered, and heaven frowns."

With these words Anna fanned the queen's love, roused hope in her dubious mind, and quelled her modest timidity. First the two visit the temples and pray for favor at the altars. Duly they sacrifice picked sheep to lawgiving Ceres and to Phoebus Apollo and to Father Bacchus, and before all to Juno, who rules the marriage bonds. Lovely Dido, holding the libation-cup in her right hand, empties it between the horns of a snow-white heifer, and she paces before the smeared altars, under the very eyes of the gods. She solemnizes the day with offerings, poring over the quivering entrails torn from the opened bodies, to learn the future's secrets. O ignorant minds of seers! What vows, what offerings, avail a woman mad with love! The fire devours her very marrow; the wound pulses silent in her breast. She burns, does unhappy Dido; she wanders, frantic, through the whole town, like a heedless deer pinned by an arrow which some shepherd in the Cretan woods has let fly and, unknowing, has left in the wound. The stricken creature flees through the groves and glades; the deadly shaft clings in her side.

Now she conducts Aeneas through her capital. She displays to him the rich, well-organized city. She begins to speak, and falters in the midst of a sentence. As the day declines she proposes another banquet; and, in her obsession, she asks to hear again the story of the Trojans' trials. And again she hangs on the words of the narrator. Then, when the guests have departed and the dim moon has followed the sun to rest and the descending stars counsel sleep, she mourns alone in the empty hall and takes the seat that he has vacated. Though they are far parted each from each, she hears him, she sees him. Possessed by love for the father, she invites the son Ascanius to her embrace, if so be she may beguile her fatal passion. The town is paralyzed; towers stand half built; the soldiers lay down their arms. The harbor defenses are stayed; all public works are suspended; and all labor stops on the huge beetling walls, topped by dizzy cranes.

When Juno, Jove's dear spouse, saw Dido in the grip of her passion, deterred by no concern for her reputation, the goddess accosted Venus with these words: "This is certainly a fine trophy, a fine achievement, of yours and your son's! It is a great and memorable feat for two gods to trick one poor woman! I am by no means blind to the fact that, in fear of my city, you have looked balefully on the high-rising houses of Carthage. But what are you aiming at? What will be the end of our disputes? Shouldn't we rather make an eternal peace by a marriage pact? You have gained what you so earnestly sought; Dido is inwardly consumed with a rage of love. Let us then assume equal authority over this people and rule it together. Let her submit to a Phrygian husband and put her Tyrians in your hand as dowry."

Recognizing that these words were insincerely uttered, in the hope of basing the promised realm of Italy on Africa, Venus countered: "Who would be so mad as to reject such terms and prefer to war against you, provided only that fortune favor the fulfillment of your proposal? But because of the Fates I hesitate, uncertain whether Jupiter wills to make one country of the Tyrians and the Trojan refugees, whether he approves the mingling of races and a political alliance. You are his wife; you can beg him to reveal his purpose. Go ahead; I will follow you."

Queen Juno replied: "I'll take that on myself. Now listen, and I'll tell you briefly how the present emergency can be met. Aeneas and poor Dido are getting ready to go hunting in the woods tomorrow, when Titan Sun first emerges and illumines the world with his rays. While the stalkers ride to and fro and set a circle of nets about the coverts I shall assail them with a black cloud heavy with hail, and I shall fill the whole sky with thunder. The huntsmen will scatter, blundering in heavy darkness; and Dido and the Trojan will find shelter in the same cave. I shall be there; and if you agree, I shall join them in connubial bonds, for good. This will be their hymen."

Venus nodded assent, without objection; she smiled at thought of the clever trick.

Now Aurora rises from Ocean's bed. And in the first dawn the young gentlemen leave the gates. They carry nets of varying mesh and broad-tipped spears. Galloping Massilian horsemen follow the keen-scented hounds. At the palace door the noblest of the Carthaginians await the queen, who has dallied in bed. Her charger, splendid in purple and gold, paws the ground and impatiently champs the bit, flecked with foam. Finally she appears, in a great cluster of attendants. She wears a Sidonian riding habit with embroidered border. Her quiver is of gold, with gold her hair is dressed, a golden clasp fastens her purple dress. The Phrygian comrades and happy young Ascanius step forth. Most handsome of all, Aeneas advances to join her; he unites his party with hers. As when Apollo leaves Lycia, his winter home, and the waters of Xanthus to visit his mother's isle, Delos, and renews the dances, while the Cretans and Dryopes and the painted Agathyrsi shout and cry; as when he climbs the Cynthian range and with soft leafage garlands his hair and binds it with gold, while the weapons clash on his shoulder—no less active than he strode Aeneas, beauty radiating from his noble face. When the expedition had reached the mountain heights and the pathless haunts of animals, wild goats, startled from their lairs at the summit, run down the slopes. Elsewhere a herd of deer scurry across, and amid clouds of dust mass their bands in flight from the mountain-tops.

Down in the valley young Ascanius rejoices in his spirited horse, and he outdistances one and all in friendly competition. He hopes to encounter among the timorous creatures a froth-dripping boar or a tawny lion dislodged from his mountain fastness.

Thereupon the whole sky began to heave and rumble mightily. A cloud heavy with hail gathered; and everywhere the Trojan heroes and their Tyrian companions and Ascanius, grandson of Venus, fearfully sought shelter in the open country; and freshets poured down from the heights. Dido and the Trojan prince discovered the same cave. Primal Earth and nuptial Juno gave the signal. Lightning supplied the marriage torches; Heaven witnessed the bridal; and the Nymphs shrieked the wedding song from the mountain peaks. That was the first day of disaster, the source of many woes. And Dido was unmoved by thought of appearances or of reputation; she conceived of no furtive love. In her eyes this was marriage, and under that name she covered her fault.

Now Rumor takes flight through the great cities of Libya—Rumor, the world's swiftest traveler. She compounds speed with speed, acquiring strength as she goes. Tiny to begin with, soon she scampers over the ground and raises her head to touch the clouds. Earth, angered against the gods, mothered her, and, they say, produced this last child, sister to Titan Coeus and Enceladus. Rumor, fleet of foot and wing, is a great horrible monster, who for every feather on her body bears a watchful eye below, and a tongue, and a roaring voice, and an attentive ear. By night she flies howling through the dark between earth and sky, nor does she close her eyes in sweet sleep. By day she perches vigilant on the rooftops or on a high tower, and much does she terrify the cities, for while clinging to the false and foul, yet she seasons it with a pinch of truth.

This creature was now filling the people's ears with discordant stories, delightedly mingling fact and falsehood. She told how Aeneas, born of Trojan stock, had arrived; how beautiful Dido thought him worthy to be her mate; and now, said Rumor, the pair are spending the livelong winter in wantonness together! Victims of lust, they forget the welfare of their countries! Such are the tales the foul goddess poured in men's ears. The stories promptly found their way to Iarbas' cognizance, and Rumor inflamed his mind with her words and stirred him to fury.

This Iarbas, son of Hammon by a Garamantian nymph he had seized, had erected a hundred temples to Jove throughout his vast realm and had consecrated ever-burning fires, eternal sentries of the gods. The ground there was greasy with the blood of sacrifices; the portals bloomed with variegated flowers. So Iarbas, distraught, infuriated by the bitter poisons of Rumor, knelt, they say, at the holy altars amid the divine presences and, his hands outstretched, prayed thus instantly to Jove: "O Jupiter Almighty, whom the Africans have learned to honor with libations when they have feasted on embroidered couches, dost thou perceive these things? Are we to feel no alarm when thou dost hurl thy jagged thunderbolts? Need we be terrified by random lightnings in the clouds? Are these cracks and rumbles meaningless? A woman who came wandering to our shores and bought the right to build a tiny city, to whom I gave plowlands and a legal lease, now has repelled my offers of marriage and has welcomed Aeneas as master in her dominions. And now that Paris with his effeminate band, with his pomaded hair and Phrygian cap and strap to hold up his chin, takes her as his spoil! And here we are, bringing useless offerings to thy temples! We are honoring, I fear, an undeserved reputation!"

The omnipotent Father heard these words from the suppliant gripping the altar; he peered down at the queen's city and at the guilty couple forgetful of their nobler fame. He called up Mercury and gave these orders: "Go, my son, summon the Zephyrs and glide on your wings down to that Trojan prince, dallying in Tyrian Carthage, unmindful of the city he is destined to found. Speak to him sharply; bring him my orders on the swift winds. Not for this did his lovely mother promise him to us. Not for this did she twice rescue him from Grecian attacks. But she vowed that it would be he who would rule Italy, quaking with war but pregnant with empire, that he would carry on the succession of the high Trojan race and subject the whole world to its laws. If the glory of such a destiny does not stir him, if he will make no effort for the sake of his own fame, does he, unnatural father, begrudge to Ascanius the high towers of Rome? What is he up to? With what treachery in mind does he linger amid that people and disregard the future Italian realm and its inhabitants? Tell him to set sail. That is my order, in a word. End of message."

He spoke. Mercury made ready to obey the Great Father. First he binds on the golden winged sandals which fly him over land and sea, swift as the wind. He takes his wand, the caduceus, in hand. This may summon pale spirits from Orcus or consign others to dismal Tartarus; it brings sleep or takes it away, and unseals the eyes in death. By its power he commands the winds and overflies the turbid clouds. Now, in his flight, he sees the summit and the steep flanks of burdened Atlas, who supports the sky on his head —Atlas, whose pine-wreathed crest is ever girt with black clouds, ever beaten with wind and rain. Snows wide and deep cover his shoulders; streams drip from his ancient chin; his bristling beard is stiff with ice. Here Cyllenian Mercury paused, balancing his wings; then he plunged straight down to the water, like a bird that skims the surface close to shore, amid the rocks where fish congregate. So Mercury, quitting his ancestor Atlas, clove the winds and flew between earth and heaven to the sandy beaches of Libya. His winged feet touched down on the seaside cottages; and immediately he perceived Aeneas superintending construction work. The Trojan bore a sword studded with yellow jaspers, and a mantle gleaming with murex and interwoven with gold thread—rich gifts of Dido.

Mercury accosted him instantly. "So now you are laying the foundations of high Carthage, and, infatuated, you are building your bride a splendid city! I am sorry to remind you that you forget your country and your fortunes! The king of the gods himself, who sways heaven and earth by his might, has sent me to you, to bring his orders through the swift air. What are you building here? To what end are you wasting idle hours in Libyan lands? If no concern for your glorious destiny moves you, if you spend your labor on futile projects, think at least of young Ascanius and the future of his hopes; for the kingdom of Italy, the Roman homeland, is his due."

After these words, Mercury's voice grew faint. In midspeech he faded from mortal sight and vanished into thin air.

Aeneas, aghast at the apparition, was dumbstruck; his hair bristled with horror, his voice stuck in his throat. Amazed at the momentous lesson, at the gods' authority, he was impelled to flee, to quit the pleasant African land. What should he do? How could he dare approach the insulted, angered queen? How could he phrase his first words to her? His mind rapidly shifted to and fro, running through every possibility. Out of his vacillation emerged at last a decision. He summoned Mnestheus, Sergestus, and stout Cloanthus, and bade them fit out the fleet and order his men to the shore, to ready their arms and keep hidden the reason for their action. Meanwhile, since dear Dido was still in ignorance and unable to grasp that their great love could be undone, he would seek her out and watch for a good chance to bring up the subject and find a way out of the mess. Cheerfully all acceded and obeyed his orders.

But *quis fallere possit amantem?* Who can fool a woman in love? The queen, fearful even when all was serene, sensed some trickery and caught a hint of the planned action. Evil Rumor, again, reported to her, aghast, that the fleet was being equipped and readied for sea-duty. Distracted, she rushed raging through the whole city, like a Thyiad, startled by the shaken emblems of the god, when, hearing the Bacchic cry, the biennial revels inspire her and at night Mount Cithaeron summons with its din.

Finally Dido perceived Aeneas, and thus charged him: "O faithless, did you hope to commit such a wicked deed and keep it secret? Could you slip away from my land without a word? Will not our love restrain you, nor our pledged word, nor the cruel death which is Dido's doom? You brute, why now are you preparing your ships in midwinter, to set sail under the northern blasts? What makes you run away to a foreign land unknown to you? If old Troy still stood, would you set forth for home on such stormy seas? Is it from me you are fleeing? By these tears, by the pledge of your hand-clasp (all that is left me, in my misery), by our union, by the unfinished rites, if I have deserved anything at your hands, or if you have found any joy in me, take pity on my crumbling home and put away this purpose of yours, I pray—if my prayers are still of any avail! On your account the Libyan people and the Numidian tyrants hate me. For you I have lost my chaste reputation and that former fame by which alone I was winning my way to heaven. I feel death coming. And what fate are you leaving me to, my guest—for what else may I call you now, since 'husband' fits no more? Why do I delay? Should I wait till my brother Pygmalion breaks down my walls, or till Iarbas the Getulian takes me captive? At least if you had given me a child before your escape, if only some little Aeneas would play in my palace halls, he would recall to me your face, and I would not seem so totally possessed, so totally abandoned."

She ceased. Aeneas, mindful of Jove's warnings, kept his eyes cast down and struggled to still the pain in his heart. At last he spoke briefly: "I shall never deny, my queen, that you have deserved of me all that you suggest; nor can any regret cloud my memory of Dido, as long as I am conscious of myself, as long as my mind controls my body. But I must say a few words in my own defense. I did not plan to escape by stealth—don't imagine it. Nor did I ever brandish the bridal torch or make a marriage compact. If the Fates had given me leave to follow my own inclinations, to soothe my sorrows by my own decisions, I should first of all have cherished the city of Troy and the sweet relics of my family. And Priam's high roofs would still remain, and I should have set up with my own hand a second Troy for the conquered. But now Grynean Apollo has ordered that broad Italy must fulfill the Lycian fates. There lies our love, there stands our destined home. If you are enthralled by the towers of Carthage and the prospect of your Libyan city, why grudge the Trojans' settling in Ausonian land? It is quite right that we should seek our country afar. Every night when the thick dark covers the land and the sparkling stars rise, the troubled ghost of my father Anchises lectures me in my dreams, and my son Ascanius reproaches me for the wrong done to him, my darling, for I would defraud him of his Hesperian kingdom and the lands assigned him by fate. And now the gods' agent, sent by Jove himself—I swear by your life and mine—has brought me my orders on the swift winds. I saw the god in bright light, within these walls. I drank in his words with these very ears. So stop exciting us both with your reproaches. It is not of my own will that I head for Italy."

As he spoke thus she had turned her head, casting wandering, uncertain glances. She looked him up and down silently; then she burst out in fury. "False, false! No goddess-mother bore you, no Dardanus fathered your race; some Caucasus gave you birth out of her sharp rocks, and Hyrcanean tigers suckled you! Why should I hide my feelings? Am I to wait for greater wrongs at your hands? Look at the fellow! Has he joined for a moment in my grief? Has he given me a kind look? Has he yielded so far as to shed a tear of pity for the one who loved him so? What can I say? Not great Juno nor Father Jupiter looks kindly upon us. Nowhere is anyone I can trust! I took you in, a castaway; in my madness I settled you in part of my kingdom. When your fleet was wrecked, I saved your party from death. And now I'm burning, I think I'm crazy! You say that now Apollo the prophet and the Lycian Fates and the gods' agent bring you on the winds their horrible orders! Ho, no doubt this is the gods' doing, this is the sort of thing that troubles their calm! Well, I am not keeping you or arguing with you. Head for Italy if you like, let the winds blow you to your kingdom overseas. I hope only that, if the good gods give heed, you will drink down your punishment, wrecked on some mid-sea rocks, and call often on the name of Dido! I'll be far away, but I'll follow you with the black torches of the Furies, and when cold death shall part my soul and body my ghost will accompany you everywhere. You are a wicked man, and you shall pay for your wickedness. I shall hear the news; it will come to me in the depths of the lower world!"

Here she broke off in the midst of speech. Sick at heart, she dropped her eyes and fled out of the sunshine, leaving him timidly hesitating, trying to formulate a reply. Her maidservants supported her tottering form, bore her into her marble chamber, and laid her on her bed.

But pious Aeneas, though longing to console the sorrowing queen and argue away her distress, nonetheless, with many a sigh and many a pang of love, obeyed the gods' orders and returned to his ships. Now the Trojans bend to their tasks; all along the shore they launch their high ships. The well-calked hulls ride the water; the men bring from the woods leafy branches to make oars; they bring ship-timbers, not waiting to shape them properly in their eagerness to be gone. There one might see them all bustling about, hurrying down from the city, as when a swarm of ants attack a great pile of grain, raiding it in mind of winter to come and storing it in their own mansions. The black army marches through the fields, carrying its booty on a narrow track through the grass. Some push the huge grains of wheat with their shoulders, some close the ranks and whip up the slackers. The whole path teems with their labors. Ah, Dido, when you saw all this, what were your feelings? Did you groan, as you looked from your high tower and saw the shores thickly crowded and the sea alive with noisy activity? O fatal love, to what do you not

condemn the human heart? *Improbe Amor, quid non mor-
talia pectora cogis?* Once again Dido is impelled to try a
last appeal, to go in tears to sway him, to beg him to yield
to love, lest she leave anything untried, and so die need-
lessly.

"Anna," she said to her sister, "you see the hurlyburly
alongshore. The Trojans have assembled from everywhere.
Now the sails are hoisted, begging a good wind; the happy
sailors have hung farewell garlands on their ships. If I have
had strength to foresee this great sorrow, I shall have
strength, sister dear, to bear it to the end. Anna, do this one
service for your wretched sister—for faithless Aeneas was
always playing up to you; he even confided to you his
secret thoughts. You are the only one who knows how and
when to approach him. Go, dear, and appeal to our proud
enemy. Say that I never joined the Greeks at Aulis in their
vow to destroy the Trojan race; I never sent ships against
Troy; I never desecrated the grave of his father Anchises,
disturbing his spirit; why then does he grimly shut his ears
to my words? What is his hurry? Will he not do a last
kindness to his unhappy adorer? Will he not await better
weather and favoring winds? I'm not asking him to renew
our alliance, which he has betrayed, nor asking that he give
up his sweet Latium and renounce his kingdom. I am just
looking to a period of repose, time for my passion to
subside, while fate may teach me how to suffer in humilia-
tion. And if he grants me this I shall not charge him with
my death."

So she spoke, and her agonized sister repeatedly carried
her woful words to Aeneas. But tears moved him not at all;
in no yielding mood would he listen to any appeals. The
Fates stood in the way; a god stopped his ears, blocked his
natural kindliness. Imagine the north winds out of the Alps
assailing a great oak, stout and long-enduring, and striving

to break it down with blasts from every quarter, and then comes a roar, and the trunk quivers and the topmost leaves are shaken to the ground, but the oak clings to the rocky soil, it sends its roots down to Tartarus as far as its summit stands in air; so is the hero assailed with high reproachful words on all sides. In his great heart he is deeply distressed. He weeps tears of pity, but his intention remains fixed.

Then unhappy Dido, terrified at her doom, prayed for death. She was sick of looking at the sky's dome. That she might the more surely fulfill her purpose and quit the light of day, it was decreed that when the sacrifices were laid on the incense-burning altars she should see the holy water turn black—a horrid sight—and the poured-out wine change to blood. No one else saw this, and she did not even report it to her sister. Now within her palace was a marble chapel dedicated to her former husband. This she held in reverence; she decorated it with snowy fleeces and festive greenery. When night covered the land she seemed to hear speech issuing thence, words in her husband's importunate voice. And solitary on the house-tops the ill-boding owl would often complain, its lingering cry changing to a wail. And many predictions of ancient seers frightened her with their ominous warnings. Heartless Aeneas haunted her feverish dreams. She seemed to be forever abandoned, alone, walking solitary down an endless road, seeking her Tyrians in some desert land. She was like mad Pentheus seeing the swarm of the Furies and a double sun and a twin of Thebes city. Or she was like Orestes in the play, son of Agamemnon, chased over the stage, fleeing his mother with her torches and black serpents, while the avenging Furies lay in wait on the doorstep.

So when, racked with anguish, she caught this madness and decided to die, she settled in secret on the time and method. Concealing her purpose under a cheery face suggesting serenity and hope, she addressed her inconsolable sister: "My dear, congratulate me! I have found a way to bring him back to me, or to break off my infatuation with him. The farthest settlement of the Ethiopians lies on the edge of Ocean, near the place of sunset. There great Atlas turns on his shoulders the heavens set with gleaming stars. A priestess of the Massilian race, come from there, has been recommended to me. She is warden of the temple of the Hesperides. There she has fed the dragon guarding the boughs of the sacred apple tree and has sprinkled his food with honey and tranquilizing poppy seeds. She professes to free, at will, troubled spirits with her spells, but to afflict others with the cruel pangs of love. She can check the flow of rivers and turn back the stars in their courses. She can call up ghosts by night. You will see the earth quake beneath her feet, and ash trees come trotting down the mountain. I assure you, dear sister, by the gods, by your own life, that I am reluctant to arm myself with magical arts. But I ask you to build, secretly, a pyre in our inner court, and lay on it our faithless hero's arms, which he left hanging up in our bedroom, and all his abandoned clothes, and our nuptial bed. The priestess directs that we must destroy all relics of the accursed man."

She lapsed into silence; a deathly pallor overspread her face. Still, it did not occur to Anna that her sister was masking her suicide under these strange rites, nor did she imagine anything more serious than the sequels to the death of Sychaeus. And so she did as commanded.

But when the pyre was built in the innermost court, open to the sky, with pine-faggots piled high and sawn ilex-logs, the queen hung the structure with garlands and crowned it with funeral wreaths. Well aware of things to come, she placed on the top Aeneas' arms, the sword he had left behind, and in the bed a figure representing him. Altars were ranged round about. The priestess, her hair flying wild, repeatedly shouted summons to the gods, to Erebus and Chaos and triple Hecate, to the three faces of virgin Diana. She sprinkled water alleged to come from the Avernal fount. She had collected juicy black plants filled with milky poison, cut by moonlight with bronze sickles. And she sought that love-charm which appears on a foal's forehead at birth, seized before its dam can snatch it away.

Dido, with loosened girdle and one foot unsandalled, stood before the altars, holding holy meal in her purified hands. Determined to die, she invoked the gods and the stars that know men's fate. Then she prayed to whatever power, righteous and regardful, cares for lovers whose passion is unrequited.

So night fell; and everywhere tired creatures were seizing their meed of soothing sleep; and the woods and the rough seas were calmed. It was the hour when the stars stand in mid-course, and all the fields are still, as are the flocks and the bright-winged birds that haunt the wide lakes and the tangled thickets. All drowse in the silent night, forgetful of their toils, assuaging their cares. Only unhappy Dido keeps vigil, never does she yield to sleep, or welcome the darkness to her eyes and heart. Her cares are redoubled, her fierce love rises and rages again, it tosses on a sea of emotion.

Thus she continues, searching her heart: "Oh, what am I to do? Shall I make overtures to my former suitors, only to be disdained? Shall I go and beg for marriage with the Numidians, whom I have so often scornfully rejected? Shall I then chase after the fleet of the Trojans, submit to them, do whatever they bid me? Should I do so, hoping that they will be grateful for my past assistance, that they abound in thankful memories? If I try to follow them, who will welcome me, even receive me, on board their proud ships? Dido, you are done for! Don't you know how faithless is the perjured race of Laomedon? Well then, what? Shall I join the crews rejoicing in their escape? Or shall I call out all my throng of Tyrians to hunt them down? Well, I was hardly able to pry my faithful people loose from Sidon; dare I order them out to sea again, to confront the tempests? No; die then, as you deserve; the sword will end all, even pain. Sister dear, it was your fault. You were moved by my tears, but you brought on the troubles that drive me mad, you exposed me to my enemy. Why could I not spend my life untroubled and innocent, unconcerned for marriage laws, like a happy animal? But as it is, I have broken my vow of fidelity to Sychaeus on his deathbed." Thus she racked her bosom with self-reproach.

Now Aeneas, sure of his departure, with all in readiness, was snatching a little sleep on the high poop of his flagship. To him came in dream a phantom of the god, looking as he had on his previous appearance, precisely like Mercury in voice and complexion, with his yellow hair and beautiful young body. The apparition seemed to deliver this message: "Goddess-born, can you sleep in this crisis? You fool, don't you see the dangerous situation you are in? Don't you hear the rustle of a favoring wind? Dido is meditating treachery, a black crime. She has made up her mind to die, and she is a prey to every evil impulse. Why aren't you running for safety, while flight is still possible? Soon you'll see the roadstead swarm with ships, incendiary torches blazing, the whole beach aflame, if dawn finds you still dawdling ashore. Ho there, snap to it! Remember, *varium et mutabile semper femina!*" So he spoke, and vanished into the dark night.

Then Aeneas, shuddering at the sudden vision, roused himself and began tongue-lashing his comrades. "Rise and shine, men! To your stations, to the rowers' benches! Shake out the sails, and smartly! A god from on high orders us, for the second time, to get going, to cut our twisted hawsers and be off! O blessed divinity, whoever you are, we are following you; once more we obey your orders, with a cheer! Guide us, serene deity, aid us, give us favoring stars!" He pulled his flashing sword from its scabbard, and slashed the mooring rope with the blade. All are filled with his contagious ardor; they seize, haul, and heave. Soon the beach is left empty, while the waters are dark with ships. The men bend to it, toss up the spray, skim over the dark-blue waters.

Now Aurora, leaving the saffron couch of Tithonus, began sprinkling the earth with the light of a new day. Queen Dido from her watch-tower saw the dawn whiten and the ships move with their sails squared away, and she realized that the shores were empty and the harbor cleared of crewmen. She beat her beautiful breast again and again and tore at her golden hair. "O Jupiter!" she cried. "Will that interloper insult my kingdom? Will not my citizens send an overwhelming force to pursue him? Won't someone launch our ships from the dockyards? Hurry! Bring firebrands, quick! Bring weapons! Run out the oars! But what am I saying? Where am I? What madness clouds my brain? O unhappy Dido, now are your own misdeeds coming home to you! You should have thought twice when you offered him the crown! Now you can judge the loyalty of him who, they say, carries the household gods of his fathers with him, of him who bore away his ancient father on his shoulders! Could I not have seized him and torn him limb from limb and thrown his remains to the waves? Could I not have killed his companions, and Ascanius himself, and served the boy up in a banquet-dish for his father? Certainly if it had come to a battle the outcome would have been uncertain. Very well; whom had I to fear in dying? I should have fired his camp, filled his tents with flame, burned alive father and son and all their race, and thrown myself headlong into the blaze! O Sun, who dost illumine all things of earth with thy beams, and thou Juno, agent and witness of my sorrows, and Hecate, whose name is shrieked by night at the crossroads, and ye avenging Furies, and ye patron-gods of dying Dido, incline your ears, let your power stoop, as is proper, to my griefs; and hear my prayers. If that villain must needs come to land and disembark, if thus Jove's Fates decree, if he is to reach that goal, yet may he be harassed by a war against a valiant race; may he be driven from his own lands and separated from Ascanius; may he beg for aid, and see the cruel massacre of his people; and when he has surrendered to the terms of a harsh peace, may he never enjoy the delights of a ruler's life, but may he fall untimely soon and lie unburied on a sandy waste! This I pray; these are my last words, while my blood still flows in my veins. O Tyrians, do you then pursue his stock and all his race to come with your hatred; lay this funeral gift on my ashes. Let there never be any love or any pact between our peoples! Arise, some avenger, from my bones! Harry the Trojan colonists with fire and sword, today, hereafter, or whenever strength is given you! Shore against shore, sea against sea, arms against arms I vow! Let there be war to the last man!"

After these words she cast about to find how she might at once end her life. She spoke briefly to Barce, the old nurse of Sychaeus (for her own nurse lay in the grave in their faraway home): "Dear nurse, please fetch sister Anna here. Tell her to hurry, to sprinkle herself with pure river-water, to bring with her sacrificial sheep and the offerings prescribed. So bid her come. And you too, bind fillets about your brow. I intend to complete the rites of nether Jove, which I have already begun, and consign to the flames the pyre of that Dardanian scoundrel."

So she spoke. The nurse bustled off with elderly alacrity. But Dido, trembling, wild with her dread purpose, with rolling bloodshot eyes and quivering fever-flushed cheeks, yet paling at the foretaste of death, rushes into the inner palace, climbs, raging, the high pyre, and unsheaths the Dardanian sword—a gift she had begged, but for no such use as this. She stopped and contemplated the Trojan clothes, the familiar bed. Pausing awhile, and weeping with awakened memories, she bent over the nuptial couch and spoke again:

"Dear relics, sweet while the Fates were kind and the gods favorable, now take my spirit with you, set me free from my sorrows. I have lived long enough. I have finished the course set me by Fortune. And now the shade of my famed person will descend to the underworld. I built an illustrious city; I saw my own walls rise. I avenged my husband, at the cost of quarreling with my brother. How happy I would have been, how more than happy, if the Dardanian ships had never even touched our shores!"

Then she kissed the nuptial bed. "Shall I die unavenged?" she cried. "Very well; at least let me die. This is the right way to end it all. May the cruel Trojan, afar on the high seas, drink in this great fire with his eyes! And may it carry to him the evil omen of my death!"

After these words the onlookers see her fall upon the sword. Blood spurts upon its blade and spatters her hands. A great shout fills the palace; and Rumor starts her wild course through the city. The roofs quake with laments and moans and the high wailing of women, the air echoes with mourning cries, as if all Carthage or ancient Troy had been overrun by foes, as if raging flames were sweeping over the roofs of houses and temples. The sister, distracted and terrified, hears the news and comes running in wild haste, tearing her face with her nails, beating her breast, and calling on the dying woman: "Sister dear, was this your purpose? Were you deceiving me? Were this pyre, these flames, these altars, prepared for me also? You abandoned me; how shall I complain of you? Dying, did you spurn your sister's company? You should have called me to the same fate! We should have died by the same blade, at the same moment! I built this pyre, I summoned the ancestral gods—and only to be cruelly absent when you so fell! O sister, you have killed me with yourself, and your people, and the city elders and all your country! Quick, let me bathe her limbs with water and catch with my lips her last wandering breath!"

While speaking thus she had climbed the lofty steps of the pyre. Moaning, she embraced and fondled her dying sister and wiped the dark blood from her dress. Dido tried to lift her heavy eyes, and again yielded. The deep wound gurgled in her breast. Three times she struggled to lift herself up on her resting-place, and three times sank back on the bed. Her wavering eyes opened, sought the light of heaven; and greeting it she fell back with a groan.

Then omnipotent Juno, taking pity on her long agony, her difficult departure, despatched Iris from Olympus to release the struggling soul from the encumbering limbs. For since Dido was dying neither in natural course nor by an external agent, Proserpina had not yet clipped the golden sacrificial lock from her head, nor had she consigned the victim to Stygian Hades. So dewy Iris descended on her saffron wings, reflecting a thousand shimmering colors against the sun, and hovered above the dying woman's head. She said: "As commanded, I take this lock, sacred to Dis; and I release you from this body." She clipped the lock; and suddenly all warmth departed from the body, and life vanished into thin air.

PYRAMUS AND THISBE
BY OVID

Publius Ovidius Naso was born at Sulmo, the present Sulmona, not far from Rome, in 43 B.C. Being possessed of comfortable means, he adopted the literary life. He stood high in favor at the court of Emperor Augustus. But he was suddenly banished in A.D. 8 or 9, no one knows just why. He spent his last dismal years at Tomi, on the western shore of the Black Sea, in what is now Bulgaria, and died in A.D. 17 or 18.

His best-known work is the *Metamorphoses*, a poetic retelling of favorite myths and legends, each involving a complete change of form, as of Chaos to Cosmos, as of Julius Caesar to a star. The spirited storytelling has commended the work to readers, and to schoolmasters, through two millennia. Three of the metamorphoses have been translated by Morris Bishop.

THIS IS the story of Pyramus and Thisbe. He was the handsomest lad, she the loveliest girl, in all the East. They lived in Babylon, that tall city which, so the story goes, Semiramis ringed with brick walls. Their houses adjoined; propinquity bred familiarity and guided them to the first stages of love. And love grew ever stronger with time. They would gladly have united in marriage, but their fathers were opposed. However, no parental veto could check their mutual ardor. They had no go-between; they could communicate only with nods and signals.

But, they say, the more a fire is confined, the hotter it burns—*quoque magis tegitur, tectus magis aestuat ignis.* There was a tiny crack in the party-wall of the two houses, remaining from the original construction. This defect had hardly been noticed for centuries. But love will find a way!

You two lovers were the first to perceive the fissure and to make of it a speaking-tube. Your endearments were transported through it securely, in gentlest murmurs. Often when they had taken their stand there, Pyramus on one side, Thisbe on the other, alternately receiving the other's breathed message, they would exclaim: "O horrid wall, what an obstacle you present to lovers! It would be so easy for you to permit our embrace! Or at least, to open wide enough for our kisses! We are not ungrateful; we admit our debt to you, that at any rate you convey our words to loving ears!" And speaking so futilely, each on his own side, they bade one another good night, and each implanted kisses doomed never to reach their destination.

One morning the dawn had snuffed the night's starry candles and the sun's rays had dried the frosty herbage, when the lovers met at their trysting-place. First they lamented their lot in low whispers. Then they agreed that they would try to give their guards the slip at nightfall, and that having once escaped from their houses they would flee out of the city, and to avoid haphazard wandering in the wide fields they would meet at the bust of Ninus and hide there in a tree's shadow. (A tall mulberry tree loaded with white fruit stood there, beside a cool spring.)

The lovers applauded the plan. Daylight, seeming to drag on forever, at last plunged beneath the waves, and from the same waters rose the night. Stealthily turning the door on its hinge, Thisbe escaped, dodging her family. Muffled in a wrap, she reached the tomb of Ninus, and sat under the appointed tree. Love had made her brave. But look! A lioness, her jaws still dripping from a recent kill of cattle, comes to slake her thirst at the nearby spring! Thisbe catches a glimpse of her in the moonlight, and fearfully takes refuge in a dark cave; and in her flight she drops her wrap. The fierce lioness, having abundantly quenched her thirst, was returning to the forest; she happened on the dropped gauzy mantle and nuzzled it with her bloody mouth.

A little late, Pyramus slipped out. He caught sight of a wild beast's tracks in the deep dust, and turned deathly pale. And when he discovered the blood-spattered garment he exclaimed: "A single night will see the end of two lovers! Of us two she best deserved a long life; the guilt lies upon my soul! I have killed you, my darling! I instructed you to come by night to this dangerous place, and I did not get here first. Now, lions who live amid these rocks, come, tear my body to pieces, devour my guilty flesh with your savage fangs! But how cowardly, merely to wish for death!"

He picked up Thisbe's mantle and carried it to the shade of the trysting-tree. He covered the beloved garment with tears and kisses. "Now drink my blood too!" he cried. He drew the sword at his side and plunged it into his bowels, and dying, withdrew it convulsively from the wound.

He lay at full length on the ground, his blood spurting high, as when, through some flaw in the lead, a pipe is cracked, and the water squirts through the tiny hole, cleaving the air, a long hissing stream. The tree's fruit, wet by the bloody spray, turned dark red; and the roots, watered with blood, tinged the hanging berries with a purple dye.

Now Thisbe returned, not yet recovered from her fright, but eager not to miss her lover. Impatiently she looked for him everywhere; she was full of the story of her escape from danger. She recognized the rendezvous and the shape of the well-known tree, but the color of the fruit gave her pause; she wondered if this was the right place. While she hesitated, she shuddered at the sight of a quivering body on the bloody soil. She took a step backward; she turned livid like boxwood, and trembled like the sea when ruffled by the breeze. But after a moment's pause she recognized her lover. She struck her guiltless arms resounding blows; she tore her hair. And embracing the beloved body, she wept upon the wounds, mingling tears with blood. And kissing the cold face she cried: "Pyramus, what calamity has taken you from me? Answer, Pyramus! Your dear Thisbe is calling you! Listen, and raise your head from the ground!"

At the name of Thisbe, Pyramus opened his eyes, already heavy with approaching death, and after a last look closed them again. Thisbe recognized her own garment, and saw the ivory scabbard empty of its sword. "Love has killed you, with your own hand, my poor sweetheart!" she cried. "My hand too is strong enough for this one deed; love too is mine. It will lend me strength to make the wound! I shall follow you to extinction; I shall be called both the wretched cause and the companion of your death. You could be parted from me by death alone; but now you cannot be taken from me even by death. O unhappy parents, mine and his, listen to our common prayer! Do not begrudge us, joined by a great love in our last hour, the privilege of burial in a single tomb. And you, O tree, who now protect one poor body with your boughs and will presently cover two, keep this remembrance of our death: forever bear dark fruit fit for mourning, the symbol of our mingled blood!"

When she had finished she poised the sword-point below her breast and fell upon the blade, still warm with death-dealing. Her vows touched the gods, as they touched the parents; for the mulberry still turns black when ripe. And all that remains of the lovers' ashes is contained in a common urn.

PHILEMON AND BAUCIS
BY OVID

This story, like the preceding one, has been translated from
the *Metamorphoses* by Morris Bishop.

O N THE Phrygian hills stands an oak beside a linden
tree, ringed by a low wall. Not far away is a swampy
lake, once habitable land, now the haunt only of marsh-
birds, coots and divers. Once Jupiter came here in mortal
form, accompanied by his kinsman Mercury the herald,
without his wings. They knocked at a thousand doors,
asking a place of repose; a thousand bolts were shot against
them. One house alone welcomed them. It was small,
roofed with straw and marsh-reeds; here pious Mother
Baucis and Philemon, equally aged, were married in youth,
and here they had grown old together. They made their
poverty light by admitting it and never grumbling. No use
looking there for distinction of master and servant; the pair
made up the whole household, both commanding and serv
ing.

When the heavenly visitors reached this humble home,
bowing their heads they entered the low door. The old
man set out a bench and told them to sit and rest their legs.
Baucis hurried to lay a coarse cloth on it. Then she stirred
the warm ashes, roused the day's fire, fed it with leaves and
dry bark, brought it to a blaze with her ancient breath,
added finely-split kindling and dry twigs from the attic,
broke them up and arranged them under her little kettle.
She took the cabbage her husband had brought in from the
well-watered garden and trimmed off its outer leaves. And
Philemon with a forked stick took down a smoke-black-

ened side of pork which hung from a beam, cut off a small slice from the long-treasured chine, and softened it in the boiling water.

Meanwhile they pass the time in talk. They shake up a mattress of soft river sedge and place it on the couch framed of willow wood. They cover it with a spread, used only on festive occasions; but this too was poor and old, in keeping with the willow bed. Thereon the gods reclined. The old woman, nervously tucking up her skirts, set the table. One of its three legs was too short; she wedged a potsherd under it. When its slope was thus corrected she wiped the surface with green mint. She laid out olives of two colors, Minerva's fruit, and autumnal cornel-berries preserved in wine-lees, and endives and radishes, and cottage cheese, and eggs, lightly scrambled on a slow fire, all served on rough earthenware. A wine-jug of the same noble material was set forth, with wine-cups whittled from beechwood, the interiors coated with yellow wax.

After a little delay the hearth contributed the hot main dishes, and wine of no great age was produced. These were removed, to give place to the second course—nuts mixed with wrinkled dates and dried figs, and plums, and fragrant apples in wide baskets, and purple grapes fresh plucked from the vines. A white honeycomb stood in the midst. And kindly faces beamed over all, nor was hearty, whole-souled good will lacking.

Suddenly they perceive that as soon as the jugs are emptied they are spontaneously refilled with wine! Baucis and shy Philemon are startled and frightened by this phenomenon. They take the attitude of prayer with upraised hands; they ask pardon for the improvised meal.

The householders had a single goose, the watchman of the little farm-house, which they then proposed to sacrifice for their divine guests. Swift of wing, he soon wore out his aged pursuers. He eluded them for some time, then took it into his head to take refuge with the gods. And these deities forbade his murder. "We are gods," they said. "Your impious neighbors will pay a well-merited penalty for their inhospitality. You will be granted exemption from their fate. Now you must abandon your home, follow in our footsteps, and climb with us to the hilltop." The old couple obeyed; leaning on their staffs they struggled to negotiate the long, steep slope.

When they had got to a bowshot's distance from the summit they looked back; they saw everything submerged in a flood, their house alone remaining. While they are staring and bewailing the fate of their friends, their old house, small even for its two occupants, is transformed into a temple. Columns replace crotched posts; the roof-thatch brightens to yellow, it seems a golden roof; the doors are richly embossed; the floor is laid with marble.

Then said Saturnian Jove, serene of visage: "Tell me, good old man, and my good woman, worthy of your honest mate, what you most desire." After a brief consultation with Baucis, Philemon voiced to the gods their common conclusion. "We pray to be your priests, to tend your shrine; and since we have lived so long and happily together, we beg that the same hour may carry off the two of us, and that I may never see my wife's tomb, and that she may never lay me in my grave."

Their prayer was fulfilled. Guardianship of the temple was theirs, as long as life lasted. Enfeebled by the weight of years, they happened at last to be standing before the sacred steps. While they were recalling the strange history of the place, Baucis perceived Philemon putting forth leaves, while Philemon saw Baucis likewise leafing. And as their faces were concealed by the gathering frondage they spoke, while still they might, their last words in unison: "Farewell, dear mate!" And the foliage hid both faces together.

Still today the Bithynians point out the two trees intertwined, side by side. This story was told me by trustworthy old men—indeed they had no reason to deceive me. I noticed votive garlands hanging from the branches. I hung one there myself, and I remarked: "Those whom the gods love are sanctified; those who have worshipped are worshipped in their turn."

PYGMALION
BY OVID

Like the preceding two, this story has been translated from
the *Metamorphoses* by Morris Bishop.

THE PROPETIDES, those filthy women, dared to disavow
the goddess Venus. Thus, smitten by her divine anger,
they were the first to prostitute their bodies and their good
name, so it is said; and thus they lost all sense of shame,
their sluggish blood would no longer rise to make their
faces blush, and they were transformed into hard stones,
images of their hearts.

Now Pygmalion had seen these women living their lives
in villainy. He was revolted by the vices which nature had
planted in the feminine mind, and so he lived long wifeless
and solitary, admitting no partner to his bed. At the same
time he masterfully carved a figure out of snowy ivory,
which no living woman could surpass; and he fell in love
with his own handiwork. She had the face of a real woman.
You would think she was alive, that she was about to move,
if she weren't restrained by modesty. Such was his art,
concealed by art! Pygmalion gazed at her, in amazement at
his own craft, and felt himself consumed with love for the
artificial creation. Often he palpated the work with searching hands, to try if it were a real body or ivory; he could
hardly admit it to be ivory. He kisses her; he thinks she
returns the kiss. He talks to her and clasps her tight. He
thinks his exploring fingers sink into her flesh; he fears that
bruises may appear on the clutched limbs. Now he over-
whelms her with endearments; now he showers her with

198 } The Romans

the gifts girls appreciate: shells and polished stones, little birds and many-colored flowers, lilies, painted balls, and amber—the tears of the Heliades dropping from trees. He clothes richly her lovely limbs, puts gemmed rings on her fingers, long necklaces about her neck. Smooth pearls adorn her ears, chaplets her bosom. All this is fine indeed, but her naked body is no less beautiful. He lays her on a bed dyed with Sidonian purple. He calls her his mistress; he poses her willowy neck on the soft pillows, as if she could feel them.

Now had come Venus' festal day, celebrated throughout all Cyprus. Heifers, their wide-spreading horns gilded, had bowed their white necks to the sacrificial blows. The altars reeked with burning incense. Pygmalion brought gifts to the shrine. Timidly he prayed: "If you gods can grant all prayers, give me, I beg, for wife"—he did not quite dare say "my ivory maid," but "one like my ivory maid." Golden Venus, who was present in person at her festival, well understood his meaning. As an omen of her divine favor, three times the altar-flame flared up and ascended into air. When he returned home he visited the image of his darling; he bent over the bed and kissed her. It seemed to him that she was warm! He kissed her again, and caressed her bosom with his hands. The ivory softened as he stroked it; the hard surface yielded, surrendering to his questing fingers, as Hymettian beeswax softens under the sunlight and under the prodding thumb accepts many forms and becomes useful by being used. The lover was overwhelmed with amazement, joy, and doubt, and fear that he was duped. Again and again he tested with his hand the response to his prayer. The body was real! The veins throbbed under his examining finger. So now our Paphian hero poured out abundant thanks, welcome to Venus. At last he pressed real living lips with his own. The maiden felt the imprint of his kisses; she blushed, and opened her timid eyes to the light. Her first glance revealed to her her lover and the sky above.

The goddess attended the bridal she had made; and when nine moons had fully waxed the girl gave birth to a daughter, Paphos, for whom the island is named.

TRIMALCHIO'S DINNER

BY PETRONIUS

The author of *Trimalchio's Dinner* was (probably) Gaius
Petronius, who throve in the early years of the first century
A.D., and who held the responsible post of proconsul of Bithy-
nia. He was more celebrated as the *arbiter elegantiæ*, the arbiter of taste, the fashionable dictator, of the court of Nero. We
know more of his death, in A.D. 66, than of his life. Expecting
arrest, he opened a vein, then rebandaged it, and conversed
with his friends light-heartedly, rewarded some slaves and
promised beatings to others, penned a denunciation of the
Emperor, reopened the vein and died elegantly, in the best of
taste.

His book, the *Satyricon*, of which only fragments remain,
is the first picaresque novel, an episodic, satiric, realistic picture
of a society seen by one of its rejected members, its inward
enemies. It is a picture of the *bohème* of a decadent world, and
a burlesque of the elegances by which Petronius lived. It is
also a burlesque of literary types: the epic, the tragedy, and
the Greek novel. And it gave literature one great enduring
character, Trimalchio himself. The translation of *Trimalchio's
Dinner* is by Morris Bishop.

[The narrator, Encolpius, his friend Ascyltus, and his boy-
friend Giton, a trio of low-life dead-beats, have somehow
wangled an invitation to dinner with the rich profiteer Trimalchio.]

Now the third day had come, bringing the prospect of
a free meal; but we had been so knocked about that
we were more inclined to sneak out of it than to wait for it.
Thus we were discussing rather sourly how to miss the
shindig, when a slave of the rhetorician Agamemnon broke
in on us. "What!" he said. "Don't you know who is giving

the party today? It's Trimalchio, society's wonder-boy! He keeps a clock in his dining-room and a bugler to sound the hours, so he'll always know how fast life is slipping away." So we immediately forgot our troubles and dressed with care. Giton freely offered to act as our slave; we told him to follow us to the baths.

There, keeping our clothes on, we strolled around, mixing with groups of sportsmen and exchanging wise-cracks. Then we noticed an old bald fellow in a red sweat-shirt playing ball with a bunch of long-haired slave-boys. It was not the boys who took our eyes—though they well deserved it—but the old gentleman in slippers tossing a green ball. When he dropped a ball he did not bother to pick it up; a slave with a sackful of balls threw out a fresh one to the players. We noticed other novelties. Two eunuchs stood at opposite sides of the ring. One held a silver chamber-pot; the other kept track of the balls, not the score of those that flew to and fro in the game, but those that fell on the floor. While we were admiring these elegances Menelaus [assistant of the rhetorician Agamemnon] ran up, to say: "This is the man who invited you. What you're seeing is just a warmup for the dinner." Menelaus had hardly stopped when Trimalchio snapped his fingers. At the signal a eunuch deftly posed the chamber-pot for the player. Having relieved himself, Trimalchio called for a basin of water, daintily dipped in his fingers, and wiped them on a slave-boy's hair.

Well, it would take too long to tell all the details. We went into the bath, and after a good short sweat we entered the cold shower. Trimalchio had been drenched in perfume; now he was having a rubdown, not with ordinary towels but with cloths of the softest wool. Meanwhile under his very eyes three masseurs were drinking his Falernian wine. Fighting over it, they spilled most of it. Trimalchio just laughed, and said they were pouring a libation to his health. Then he was wrapped in a scarlet bathrobe and placed on a litter. Four liveried footmen wearing cockades preceded him, also a small cart transporting his favorite, a little old fellow with bleary eyes, even uglier than his master. As Trimalchio was carried out his flute-player joined him, and played all the way on a pocket mouthorgan, as if he was tootling a confidential message in the master's ear.

Filled with wonder, we followed along, together with Agamemnon. We reached Trimalchio's house door, which bore this notice: "Any slave who leaves the house without his master's permission will receive 100 lashes." In the porter's lodge stood the doorman in a green livery with a cherry-colored sash; he was shelling peas into a silver dish. Over the door hung a golden birdcage, in which was a spotted magpie, saluting the guests.

While I was looking at everything in amazement, I started and nearly fell and broke a leg. On the wall on our left at the entrance, not far from the porter's room, was a huge painted dog, chained up, and over him a big sign, in capitals: BEWARE OF THE DOG. My companions laughed at me; I collected my wits and took a good look at the whole wall. The fresco represented a slave market, the merchandise lined up and wearing price-cards. Then came Trimalchio himself, long-haired, carrying a wand, entering Rome under the guidance of Minerva. The realistic painter had showed in detail, and with explanatory inscriptions, how the slave had learned bookkeeping and had finally become steward. At the end of the portico wall Mercury appeared, lifting him up by the chin and setting him on the bench of a high tribunal. There was Fortune also with her horn of plenty, and the three Fates twisting their golden threads. I noticed also in the portico a group of runners practicing with a trainer. And I observed in a corner a big cupboard containing a small shrine with silver statuettes of the Lares and a marble Venus, and also a good-sized gold casket preserving, according to report, Trimalchio's first beard. I asked the houseman what the pictures in the middle represented. "The *Iliad* and the *Odyssey*," he replied, "and a big gladiatorial show put on by Laenas." But we didn't have time to examine these in detail.

Now we had got to the triclinium, or dining-room. At the entrance the steward was going over his accounts. I was especially struck by the fasces, rods and axes, affixed to the doorposts. These were supported on what seemed to be a ship's ram, in brass, with the inscription: "To Gaius Pompeius Trimalchio, Augustal municipal counselor, from his steward Cinnamus." Under this label hung a double lamp. There was a tablet on each doorpost, like a bulletin board. If I remember correctly, one of the notices read: "On the 30th and 31st of December our master, Gaius, dines out." The other doorpost bore a chart of the moon's and the seven planets' courses, with a set of knobs indicating the lucky and unlucky days.

Sated with these delights, we were about to step into the dining-room when one of the slaves, posted there for the purpose, shouted: "Right foot first!" Naturally we stopped short, for fear someone would cross the threshold against the rules. As we all stepped out together with the right foot forward, a naked slave threw himself at our feet and implored us to save him from punishment. The offense which had brought him into jeopardy was no great matter; he had let someone at the baths steal the steward's clothes, hardly worth ten sesterces. So we drew back our right feet and begged the steward, who was still counting money in the atrium, to remit the slave's punishment. He raised his head haughtily, and said: "It isn't the loss of the money I mind so much as the carelessness of the worthless slave. He lost my dinner clothes, which one of my clients gave me for my birthday. Tyrian dye too, naturally. But they have already been washed once. Well, it's a small matter. I'll let him off as a favor to you."

So at last we took our places. Alexandrian slaves poured iced water on our hands. Others followed, specialists, who trimmed our toenails very skilfully. They didn't do their rather disagreeable task in silence; they sang all the time. I was curious to find out if the whole corps of slaves were singers, so I asked for a drink. A slave popped up and filled my order with a shrill singsong. All the other requests were honored in the same way. You would have thought it a theatrical performance rather than a family dinner.

All had now taken their places except Trimalchio himself. (According to the new fashion the highest couch was reserved for him.) The hors d'oeuvre were very elegantly served. On the relish tray stood a donkey of Corinthian bronze equipped with two baskets, one filled with white olives, the other with black. Two dishes were set out beside the ass; they were marked with Trimalchio's name and the weight of the silver. Metal containers shaped like bridges offered dormice in honey, sprinkled with poppy-seeds. Sausages were presented hot on a silver grill, with a bed of sliced damson plums and pomegranates below.

While we were sampling these dainties Trimalchio himself was carried in, to music. He was propped up on a pile of little cushions, and provoked a smile from incautious guests, for his shaven head stuck out from his scarlet robe, and he had wrapped his neck, already muffled in scarves, in a napkin with a broad royal-purple stripe and dangling fringes. He had also a large gilt ring on the little finger of his left hand, and on the top joint of the next finger a smaller ring; it looked to me like solid gold [forbidden to commoners], but evidently it was studded with twinkling steel stars. And for fear that he wasn't sufficiently displaying his prosperity, he left his right arm bare, to show off a gold bracelet and an ivory bangle trimmed with dazzling metal. Picking his teeth with a silver toothpick, he addressed us: "My friends, I really wasn't yet ready to come to table, but not to deprive you longer of my company, I gave up my own pleasure. But certainly you will permit me to finish my game." A slave followed him carrying a checkerboard of juniper wood with checkers of crystal. I noticed one very neat refinement: instead of the white and black counters he used silver and gold coins. Incidentally, during the game he descended to all sorts of low expressions.

While we were still enjoying the canapés, a tray was brought in bearing a wooden hen spreading her wings wide, as if she were setting. Two slaves stepped up, and keeping time to loud music began to poke about in the straw. They pulled out some peahens' eggs, which they distributed among the guests. Trimalchio watched this performance and exclaimed: "My friends, I ordered peafowls' eggs to be put under the hen; but by Hercules I'm afraid they've begun to develop. Well, let's try them anyhow; maybe we can still suck them!" Spoons weighing at least half a pound each were passed around, and we tapped the eggs, which were made of rich pastry. The fact is, I was on the point of throwing my share away, for I thought it real and already turning into chicken. Then I heard a guest, an old hand at these parties, remark: "I'll bet there's something good inside!" So I cracked the shell with my hand and found inside a fine fat beccafico, the fig-eating bird, rolled up in peppered egg-yolk.

Now Trimalchio had at last finished his game. He demanded his share of all the dishes served up, and proposed in a loud voice that anyone who wished could have a second drink of mead. At a sign from the musicians the hors d'oeuvre were carried out by a troop of singing waiters. In the confusion a silver side-dish was carelessly dropped. The slave bent to pick it up from the floor. Trimalchio noticed it; he ordered that the slave should have his ears boxed and the dish be thrown down again. A houseboy rushed in with a broom and swept up the silver dish along with the rest of the table scraps. Then two long-haired Ethiopians entered with little leather bottles, like the flunkeys who sprinkle the sand in the circus with perfume. They poured wine over our hands; no water was in evidence.

We duly applauded our host's magnificent refinements. "Mars likes everything to be fair and square," he said. "So I have ordered that everyone is to have a table to himself. Anyhow, the filthy slaves won't bother us so much by squeezing in among us."

Then glass wine-jugs, carefully sealed, were brought in. Each had a label about its neck, with this legend: "Falernian of the consulship of Opimius. Guaranteed 100 years old." While we were perusing the inscription Trimalchio clapped his hands and cried: "Alas, wine lives longer than wretched man! So drink it down! Life is wine, or rather, wine is life! I'm giving you the real Opimian. Yesterday I didn't bring out such good wine, although my guests were far more important."

While we were drinking and admiring the various *articles de luxe* a slave trundled in a silver skeleton, constructed so that the limbs and backbone could be twisted and turned in any direction. This was tossed on the table several times; its movable jointings permitted it to assume a number of striking poses. Trimalchio chimed in:

What is man? Why, nothing at all!
And when we answer the final call
We'll be in that same circumstance;
So let us live, while we got the chance!

We all applauded loudly.

The course that followed was rather a let-down, but it was novel enough to capture our attention. A round tray was marked with the twelve signs of the zodiac in a circle; on each of them the chef had placed appropriate titbits. Upon the Ram he had put ram's-head chickpeas; upon the Bull a slice of beef; upon the Twins a pair of lamb's fries with kidneys; upon the Crab a garland; upon the Lion an African fig; upon the Virgin a bit of sowbelly; upon the Scales a balance with a pastry twist on one side, a cheesecake on the other; upon the Scorpion a seafish; upon the Archer a hare; upon Capricorn a lobster; upon Aquarius a goose; upon the Fish two mullets. In the midst [no doubt representing Earth] a patch of grassy turf supported a honeycomb. An Egyptian slave brought around bread in a silver warming-pan, at the same time murdering a song from the pantomime *Asafœtida*. We set to, rather sulkily, on the commonplace food. But "Let's eat!" said Trimalchio. "Dig in! This is just the beginning." Then four waiters danced in to music and removed the upper layer of the tray, revealing underneath capons and sowbellies and in the middle a hare equipped with wings, to represent Pegasus. We noticed also at the corners four statuettes of Marsyas, with spicy garum-sauce trickling down from their bellies onto the fish swimming in a little fishpond. We all joined in applause, initiated by the slaves, and, laughing, we attacked the delicacies. Trimalchio was more pleased than anyone by the success of this conceit. He began to shout: "Carver!" A carver stepped up, and slashed at the dainty morsels to music, in ballet style; you would have thought him a singing gladiator enacting a fight to the accompaniment of a water-organ. Nonetheless Trimalchio kept muttering: "Carver! Carver!" Suspecting that this repetition had something to do with a joke, I ventured to question a convive. He had often watched such performances. He replied: "You see the man who is cutting up the victuals? His real name is Carver; so whenever Trimalchio says: 'Carve 'er, Carver!' he's using both the imperative of the verb and the vocative of the noun."

I couldn't take another bit, so I turned to my companion to get filled in on the facts. I gave him a good line about myself; and I asked who the woman was who was running all over the place. "Why, she's Trimalchio's wife, Fortunata! And well named; she's loaded. And yesterday what was she? If you'll excuse the expression, you wouldn't have taken a bit of bread from her fingers. And now, God knows how or why, she has landed right and she's Trimalchio's baby doll. If she told him it was midnight at noon he'd believe her. He has no idea how much he's got; he's rolling in the stuff. But that bitch keeps her eye on everything; you'd be surprised. She stays sober and talks sense, but she can tear you to pieces, and she'll show you who's boss. If she likes you she likes you; but if not, not." . . .

[Trimalchio explains, ridiculously, the symbolism of the astronomical dish.]

While we were acclaiming our host's learning, servants appeared and draped the couches with coverlets embroidered with hunting-nets and hunters with spears and all the implements of the chase. We didn't know what was in preparation, until a great uproar burst forth in the next room, and suddenly some Spartan hounds erupted and began running around our tables. They were followed by men with a large salver, on which reposed an enormous wild boar wearing a liberty cap. From its tusks depended two small baskets of palm-leaves, one filled with Syrian, the other with Theban dates. Around it were placed tiny piglets of cake-dough, as if they were snuggling up to the teats, implying that the boar was a female. The piglets were favors to take home. The person who stepped up to dismember the boar was not Carver, who had operated on the capons, but a big bearded man wearing hunter's leggings and a rough outdoorsman's cape. He drew his hunting-knife and struck the boar a mighty blow, whereat some thrushes flew out of the gash. But birdcatchers armed with limed sticks had been provided. They soon captured the birds fluttering about the room. Trimalchio ordered that one be given to each guest, remarking: "Now you see what fine acorns that wild boar fed on." Immediately the slaves took the baskets hanging from the boar's tusks and divided the dried and fresh dates among the guests.

Meanwhile I had wondered off in a train of speculation, wondering why the boar had worn a liberty cap. After exhausting my fond fancies I determined to ask my informative neighbor why. Said he: "Even your own slave could answer that one. It's obvious enough, no puzzle. This boar was served yesterday as the main dish, but the dinner guests were so full they couldn't touch it; and so today he comes to dinner as a freedman." I cursed my stupidity and put no more questions, for fear of appearing a lout who had never dined with the upper crust.

While we were talking a beautiful slave-boy, garlanded with vine-leaves and ivy, impersonated Bacchus, or Liber, in his various aspects, passing around grapes in a basket and reciting his master's poems in his piping voice. Trimalchio turned round at this and exclaimed: "Liber Bacchus, receive your liberty!" The boy pulled the liberty cap off the boar and clapped it on his own head. Trimalchio added: "You won't deny that I'm the original Mr. Liberator!" We all applauded Trimalchio's joke and kissed the boy soundly as he made his rounds.

After this course Trimalchio rose and went off to the toilet. . . .

Trimalchio returned. . . . We didn't yet realize that we were only halfway up the Hill of Plenty, as the poets say. For when the tables had been cleared, to a musical accompaniment, three live white pigs were brought in, equipped with muzzles and bells. The maître d' said one was two years old, one three, one six. I thought that some performers would then enter and put the pigs through their tricks, as they do before street crowds. But Trimalchio proved me wrong. "Which of these pigs do you want for dinner?" he inquired. "Any farm-cook can whip up a fowl, or a Pentheusburger,* or any such trifle. But my cooks often boil a calf whole in the copper boiler."

On the spot he ordered up the chef, and without waiting for our vote told him to kill the biggest one. "Which corps do you belong to?" he asked loudly. "To the fortieth, sir," replied the chef. "Were you bought or born on the estate?" "Neither, sir," said the cook. "I was left to you in Pansa's will." "Well, see you do your job well, otherwise I'll have you put on the road gang."

The cook, being thus reminded of his master's power, led the pig off to the kitchen. . . .

While our host was still talking, a dish with an immense pig was laid on the table. We were amazed at the chef's speed; we swore he couldn't have cooked a chicken so fast, all the more as the pig seemed much bigger than the wild boar we had just had. Trimalchio inspected it more and

* Pentheusburger: Pentheus, king of Thebes, was chopped small by the Maenads, or Bacchantes.

more closely, and then cried out: "What's this? What's this? Hasn't this pig been gutted? No, by God, it has not! Call up that cook right away!"

The chef was summoned; he stood woebegone before the table and said he had forgotten to clean the beast. "What! Forgotten!" Trimalchio exclaimed. "You'd think he'd just forgotten to pepper and salt it! Strip him!"

Without a moment's delay the cook was stripped. He stood mournfully between two guards, the household torturers. The guests tried to put in a good word for him. "These things do happen," we said. "We beg you, do let him off. If he ever does it again, none of us will say a word for him." Personally, I was much more inclined to severity. I couldn't help leaning over and whispering in Agamemnon's ear: "This slave must be about as bad as they come. How could anyone forget to gut a pig? I wouldn't overlook it if he failed to clean a fish." But Trimalchio simply sat there with a great grin all over his face. "Well," he said, "since your memory's so bad, you can just do the gutting right here in front of us." The cook was given back his tunic; he took a knife and hesitantly cut here and there on the porker's belly. And out of the cuts, thanks to the internal pressure, gushed sausages and black puddings.

After this stunt all the slaves applauded, shouting: "Hurrah for Trimalchio!" The chief was honored with a silver crown and a goblet of drink, presented on a tray of Corinthian bronze. When Agamemnon took a close look at it, Trimalchio said: "I'm the only one who has the genuine Corinthian." I expected that, bragging as usual, he would say that he had his bronze ware imported specially from Corinth. But he was one up on me. "If you want to know how I'm the only one to possess the real Corinthian, it's because the craftsman I buy it from is named Corinthus. And what is Corinthian, if not something made by Corinthus? And I'm not so dumb; I know very well the origin of Corinthian ware. When Troy fell, Hannibal, who was a smart scalawag, piled up all the statues, gold, silver, and bronze, on a great bonfire and melted them down. So they were all fused together in one bronze amalgam. Then the metal-workers pulled out the material from this mass and made platters and serving dishes and statuettes of it. That's how Corinthian ware began, everything mixed up together, neither this nor that. Pardon me if I say I prefer glass; at any rate it doesn't smell. If it didn't break so easily, I'd like it better than gold. And now glass is very cheap.

"You know, there was a workman once who made an unbreakable glass bowl. He got in to see Emperor Tiberius and presented his gift, and then he asked the Emperor to hand it back, and he threw it on the floor. The Emperor was in a frenzy. But he picked up the bowl; it was just dented like a brass bowl. He pulled a little hammer out of his pocket and calmly tapped it into shape. Then he thought he was floating on a cloud, the more so when Caesar said to him: 'Does anyone else know how to make this kind of glass?' Now listen to this. He said there was no one. 'Off with his head!' ordered Caesar, remarking that if the secret was known we'd think no more of glass than of mud." . . .

[Various floor shows enliven the eating and drinking.]

A troupe of choral singers entered, and clashed their spears against their shields. Trimalchio raised himself up on his cushion, and when these Homerists recited the poetry in Greek, as they do in their highflown way, he read in a bellow out of a Latin book. When they came to a stop he said: "Do you know what the story's about? Well, there were two brothers, Diomede and Ganymede, and they had a sister named Helen. And Agamemnon ran away with her and left a deer in her place, to fool Diana. Then Homer tells of the great war between the Trojans and the Grojans. Homer won, and married his daughter Iphigenia to Achilles. So naturally Ajax went insane. But here he is; he'll explain the plot himself."

At this the choral speakers raised a shout. The slaves rushed about; and a calf, boiled whole, was brought in on a giant presentation tray; it was even wearing a helmet. Ajax then appeared; he drew his sword, and waved it about as if crazy. He then cut up the veal, now with the edge, now with a broadside blow. He speared the chunks with the point and distributed them among the marvelling guests.

We didn't have much time to admire these elegant inventions, for suddenly the roof began to rumble and the whole dining-room shook. I was terrified; I started up in fear that some acrobat would fall through the roof. All the other guests stared upward in amazement, expecting some portent from heaven. But behold! Two panels of the ceiling parted and a big hoop, no doubt off a hogshead, was let down. It was all hung with golden crowns and alabaster perfume-vials. We were told to take these home as favors. I looked back at the dinner-table. A tray of cheese-cakes had been deposited there. In the middle stood a Priapus made of pastry, supporting an apronful of fruits and grapes in his usual vulgar way. We all reached out our hands eagerly for the dainties; then suddenly a fresh novelty made us laugh again. For if we barely touched the cakes and fruits they squirted out a saffron scent, the spray unpleasantly spattering our faces. Naturally we thought that the use of sacred saffron indicated some religious rite, so we sprang to our feet and shouted: "Hail to the Emperor, Father of his Country!" After this solemn moment some of us snatched the fruit and rolled it up in our napkins. . . .

Trimalchio gave an imitation of a bugler, and then looked around for his favorite slave, whom he called Croesus. This creature had bleary eyes and rotten teeth. He was busy wrapping up a black, disgustingly fat lap-dog in a green cloth, setting a half loaf of bread on the couch beside him and trying to stuff it into the mouth of the poor animal, who was on the point of throwing up. Noticing this, Trimalchio ordered in Buster, "protector of house and household." Promptly an enormous beast was led in on a chain; a kick from his handler persuaded him to lie down. Trimalchio tossed him a bit of white bread; "nobody in the whole house loves me so much," he proclaimed. The favorite slave, annoyed at the praise of Buster, set his lap-dog on the floor and sicked him on to give battle. Buster, in canine fashion, filled the room with horrible barks and nearly tore Croesus' "Little Pearl" to pieces. As if a dog-fight weren't enough, in the hurlyburly a chandelier on the table was knocked over, breaking drinking-glasses and spraying the guests with hot oil. To show he was not upset by the losses, Trimalchio kissed his favorite and told him to climb on his back. The slave rode his steed piggyback, slapped his shoulders with his open hands, and cried: "Buck, buck, how many are up?" * Then Trimalchio calmed down and ordered a big bowl of punch mixed and served out to the slaves, who were sitting at our feet. He added: "If anyone declines it, pour it on his head. Business by day, fun by night.". . .

---

* *Bucca, bucca, quot sunt hic?* A friend of the editor's, raised in Boston, recalls a boyhood game, in which one boy stood behind another and demanded: "Buck, buck, you lousy muck, how many hands have I got up, one, two, or none?"—a remarkable example of folkloric and linguistic persistence, through two millennia and across half a world.

[The feast continues. The overstuffed guests are revolted by the succession of pretentious dishes. Trimalchio turns quarrelsome and fights with his wife. He recounts his own rise from slavery to opulence. He develops a crying jag; and addresses a slave.]

"Stichus, bring out the toga which I intend to be buried in, and bring out too the perfume and a taste of the wine, out of the big jar, in which my bones are to be washed, by my order."

Stichus dashed off. He returned with a white sheet and an official's toga. Trimalchio asked us to feel the quality of the wool. Then he said with a smile: "Look here, Stichus, don't let any mice or moths get at it, or I'll have you burned alive. I want to be carried off in style, so that the whole city will pray for me." Then he opened a flask of spikenard and anointed us all with a bit. He said: "I hope I'll like the smell as well when I'm dead as I do when I'm alive." He ordered some wine poured in the mixing-bowl. "Just imagine you're all guests at my funeral," he said.

All this was getting very unpleasant. Trimalchio, now drunk as a lord, thought of a new diversion. He ordered a brass band sent in; and, propped up on a pile of cushions, he stretched out on the couch. "I'm dead," he said. "Now say something nice about me." The bank struck up a funeral march. A slave of the undertaker, that very respectable man, blew such a mighty blast that he woke up the whole neighborhood. The local fire-brigade, thinking the house was on fire, suddenly crashed in the door and poured in, flourishing their axes and sloshing their fire-buckets in a general tumult. We seized the opportunity; we ditched Agamemnon and dashed out as if escaping from a real fire.

THELYPHRON'S STORY
BY APULEIUS

Lucius Apuleius was born about A.D. 125 in the city of
Madaura, a colony of Roman army veterans in North Africa,
near the present frontier of Tunisia and Algeria. He studied
in Carthage, Athens, and finally Rome, before settling in
Carthage. There he lectured on philosophy and rhetoric and
filled public offices. The date of his death is not known.

A dilettante cosmopolite intellectual, he wrote *The Golden
Ass* for fun. It is the only surviving example of the Latin novel,
besides Petronius' fragmentary *Satyricon*. His sophisticated
storytelling, comic sense, and command of stylistic effects suggest that Latin prose fiction had already developed its own
forms and devices. Our translations from *The Golden Ass* are
by Morris Bishop.

[The narrator, Lucius (Apuleius' own name), is traveling
in Thessaly, in northern Greece. He comes to the town of
Hypata and visits a kinswoman, Byrrhaena. She invites him to
supper.]

I FOUND there a number of guests, indeed the *crème de la
crème* of society, as Byrrhaena was the town's first lady.
The tables glittered with inlaid citron-wood and ivory, the
couches were spread with cloth of gold; the wide cups,
though all different, were all equally rich and pretentious.
Here stood a goblet daintily engraved, and another of flaw-
less crystal, and table-settings of bright silver and gold, and
hollowed-out amber, and precious stones cut to make drink-
ing-vessels, and everything you would hardly have believed
possible. A number of waiters in fine liveries deftly served
the bountiful dishes; and curly-headed pages, handsomely
costumed, plied us with old wine in cups, each made of a

single precious stone. Lights were brought in; the room was a noisy hubbub of talk, with shouts of laughter, risqué jokes, and familiar mockeries.

Byrrhaena turned to me, saying: "And how do you like our town? In my opinion, we're ahead of them all in our temples, baths, and suchlike, and our table-ware is quite famous. The *rentier* is not troubled; the businessman finds crowds of customers, almost as in Rome; and the average man enjoys rural peace. In fact, we are the pleasure-resort of the whole province."

I replied: "You are quite right. I have never found myself freer in my actions than I have been here. But I am terrified by the dark, evil dens where magic lurks. For they say that not even the tombs of the dead are inviolate, but ghouls ransack the graves and pyres for scraps and slices of the deceased, to use for malignant spells against the living. And as soon as the old witches hear of a funeral they come in a flash to do their dirty work before the body is laid in the grave."

At this another guest spoke up: "That is quite true. And even the living are not safe. I know a man—I won't mention his name—who had such an experience and ended up with a dreadfully mutilated face."

Thereat all the guests burst into unmannerly laughter. They turned to look at an individual who was sitting alone in a corner. He was embarrassed by the attention paid him; he muttered angrily as if determined to walk out. But Byrrhaena said: "Now, now, my dear Thelyphron, sit still a while, be nice and tell your story, so that Lucius, dear boy, may have the pleasure of hearing the thrilling tale."

He replied: "You, dear lady, are always kind and gracious; but the insolence of some people is not to be endured." He was obviously much agitated; but Byrrhaena persisted, urged him for his own ease of mind to speak, and persuaded him, despite his reluctance, to tell his story. He plucked together the couch-covers, rested his elbow on them, sat up straight, thrust out his right hand, and in oratorical style curled in the third and fourth fingers while extending the others upward, with the thumb in threatening pose. He began:

When I was a young man I went from Miletus to see the Olympic games; and as I wanted to see the sights of Thessaly I traveled all through this famous province, until I came in an evil hour to Larissa. Now in my peregrinations my funds had run rather low and I was looking for some remedy for my poverty. Then I noticed in the middle of the forum a tall old man, standing on a stone and proclaiming in a loud voice that if anyone would stand guard over a dead body he would be well paid. I said to a bystander: "What's all this? Do dead men fly away in this town?"

"Better keep your mouth shut!" said he. "You're very green and a stranger here. You don't realize you're in Thessaly, where the witches bite off the faces of the dead, to use as material for their black arts."

"Tell me, my friend," said I, "what this corpse-guarding consists of."

"Well," said he, "first you must hold a very sharp watch all night; you must keep your eyes fixed and unwinking, never looking or even glancing aside; for these horrid witches can turn themselves into whatever animal they choose, so that they can easily cheat the very eye of the sun or of Justice itself. They can take the form of birds or dogs or mice, even of flies. Then they will put the watchers to sleep with their unholy charms. No one can tell what tricks these wicked women will contrive to satisfy their evil lusts.

And yet the pay offered for this dangerous job is no more than four to six gold pieces. Oh yes, there is one thing I had almost forgotten—if the guard does not turn over the body sound and whole in the morning, and if any bits have been cut off, he must suffer the same amputations to be made from his own face, to provide replacements."

When I heard this I plucked up my nerve and went up to the crier. "Stop the announcement!" I said. "I'm your watchman. What do I get?"

"A thousand sesterces," said he. "You'll get your pay. But look here, young man, you must very carefully protect the body from the evil harpies. The deceased is the son of one of our leading citizens."

"Stop your nonsense," said I. "Don't you worry. I'm the original iron man. I never sleep. I'm all eyes; I can see better than lynx-eyed Lynceus or hundred-eyed Argus."

Immediately then the crier took me to a certain house. As the main doors were shut he brought me to a small back entrance. Then he summoned me into a dark room, with the shutters closed. He indicated to me a matron, in tears, and dressed in a black gown. He went up to her and said: "This man has undertaken to keep faithful vigil over your husband." She thrust aside the mass of hair hanging down, revealing a face lovely even in its grief. She looked me up and down; all she said was: "See that you do your duty with the utmost vigilance."

"Put your mind at ease," said I, "especially if you pay me a little extra." She agreed; and then rose and led me into another room. There lay the body wrapped in snowy sheets. Then seven witnesses were brought in. She uncovered the body and wept some time over it. Then she pointed meticulously to the features, and called the seven to attest a memorandum, which one of them carefully wrote down. "Here is the nose, entire," she said, "the eyes untouched, the ears complete, the lips perfect, the chin whole. My good citizens, take careful note." This was all recorded and signed by the witnesses.

"Madam," said I, "please order all the things necessary for my vigil."

"And what are they?" said she.

"A big lamp, and oil enough to last till morning, and wine-jugs and warm water, and a cup, and a dish of left-overs from your dinner."

She shook her head. "Get out, you fool!" she said. "You ask for a dinner, or leftovers, in a house of mourning, where for many days not even a fire has been lit! Do you think you have come here for a party? Why don't you weep and wail, suitably to the circumstances?" But while saying this she caught the eye of a servant-girl. "Myrrhine!" she said; "Fetch a lamp and oil right away, then leave the room and lock in the watcher."

So I was left alone to bear the corpse company. I rubbed my eyes to keep them ready for the watch, and roused up my spirits by singing. Twilight fell, and night grew darker and darker, till came pitch-black midnight. Well, I got more and more nervous, I admit. Then suddenly a weasel crept in and stopped in front of me and stared at me fixedly. I was really disturbed by the audacity of such a tiny creature; so finally I said: "Get out, you filthy beast! Go and hide among your fellows, the rats, before you feel the weight of my hand! Get out!" It turned and ran, and left the room empty.

And then I was plunged into the deepest abyss of sleep, so that Apollo himself could hardly have told which of the two recumbent bodies was the more dead. I lay unconscious, needing a guard myself; I might as well not have been there at all.

But at length the crowing cocks announced the end of

night. I woke, and gripped by terror I ran to the body, lamp in hand. I pulled back the winding-sheet and examined the features. They were all intact!

Then the wretched wife entered, weeping and agitated, with the witnesses of the previous day. She threw herself on the corpse and kissed it long and ardently. Then she inspected it with the lamp and found it whole. She turned back and summoned her steward, Philodespotus; she ordered him to pay the faithful guard his fee. Thereupon she said: "I thank you heartily, young man; and, I swear, you have been so scrupulous that I'll consider you henceforth as one of the family." I was standing there beaming with joy at my unexpected windfall and caressing the shining gold pieces incredulously. I replied: "Indeed, Madam, consider me your most humble servant; and if ever you desire my services, command me in all confidence."

This was a blunder. I had no sooner uttered these equivocal words than the servant corps, shocked at the suggestion, rushed at me with the weapons nature had given them. One punched my face, another poked my back with his elbows, others slapped my sides, kicked me, pulled my hair and tore my clothes. So I was mishandled like haughty young Adonis or Orpheus, the Muses' bard, and I was driven from the house in sad disarray.

I fled to a nearby square to recover my spirits; and I recalled, too late, my unconsidered, ill-omened words, and I judged myself worthy of even a worse beating than I had received.

Now the dead man, after the proper tributes and lamentations, was brought forth. As he was one of the prominent citizens, he was carried through the forum in a pompous funeral procession, according to the local custom.

Then an old man, dressed in mourning, weeping bitterly

and tearing his venerable gray hair, clasped the coffin in his arms, and cried in a strangling voice, broken by sobs: "I pray you, citizens, for the sake of your honor and civic justice, halt the interment of our dead companion, and sternly avenge a horrible crime, by punishing that wicked woman, its author! For she alone, and none other, poisoned that wretched young man, my sister's son, to facilitate her adultery and obtain his estate!" Thus did the old man cry his grievous accusations into the ears of each and all. He roused the anger of the crowd, swayed by the mere likelihood of the deed to believe in the crime. Men cried out that the wife should be stoned and burned; they urged the street urchins to begin the massacre. But she, with feigned tears and great oaths, called all the gods to witness that she was innocent of any such crime.

Then said the old man: "Let us entrust the determination of the truth to divine providence. Here stands Zatchlas the Egyptian, first of soothsayers, who long since made a pact with me, for a great fee, to bring back this man's soul briefly from the lower world, and reanimate his body when beyond death's threshold." Thereupon he thrust forth a young man with a shaven head, wearing a linen gown and palm-leaf sandals. The old man kissed his hands fervently and embraced his knees. "Have mercy, O priest!" he said. "Have mercy! By the stars in heaven, by the infernal powers, by the elements of nature, by the night's silence, by the Coptic temples, by the rise and fall of the Nile, by the secrets of Memphis, by the sacred rattles of Isis, recall the dead man briefly to broad day, and pour a little light upon his eyes, forever to be closed. We do not defy fate, nor do we deny to earth its due; we beg only a moment of life, that he may have the satisfaction of seeing justice done."

The seer, thus adjured, placed a certain small herb on the dead man's lips and another on his breast. Then he turned to the east and made a silent prayer to the glorious rising sun. The crowd, spellbound by his solemn performance, awaited the promised miracle.

I infiltrated the throng and, standing on a large stone behind the bier, I watched everything with eager interest. The corpse's breast heaved, blood began to run in the veins, and breath stirred the body. The dead youth sat up and spoke: "Why do you call me back to the duties of this fleeting life, when I have already drunk from the Lethean cup and floated on the Stygian marsh-waters? Cease, I beg you; cease; and leave me to my rest!"

These were the corpse's words. But the seer, somewhat angrily, cried out: "Why do you not tell the people all? Why do you not reveal the secret of your death? Don't you realize that I can call up the Furies by my spells, and torture your tired limbs?" Then the figure again raised its head from the bed, uttered a deep groan and addressed the throng: "I perished by the evil arts of my newly wedded wife; poisoned by her, I surrendered my bed, still warm, to an adulterer."

Then this admirable wife collected her wits and denied his charges, arguing violently and sacrilegiously. The excited populace were of two minds; some proposed burying the wicked woman alive with her husband; others put no trust in the presumed lies of the dead man. But the young man's next words extinguished doubt. Heaving another deep groan, he said: "I shall give you evidence of the absolute truth; I shall reveal to you what no man has ever hitherto known." He pointed his finger at me, and continued: "When this clever guard of my body was keeping close watch over me, the old witches hovered near to despoil me. They took on strange forms, in vain; they were baffled by the sharp watch he kept. Then they wrapped him in a cloud of sleep, making him totally unconscious. Then they called me by name; and my drugged limbs and cold members struggled to respond to the magic command. And when he too, though alive and merely dead to the world, heard my name called—which is Thelyphron, the same name as his—he answered unconsciously to the summons, and walked obediently in a trance, like a ghost. And though the door of the room was carefully locked, the witches entered through some tiny hole and cut off first his nose and then his ears. Thus he suffered a butchery intended for me. And to disguise the consequences of their crime they modelled artificial wax ears exactly like those that had been cut off, and built up a nose, a perfect copy of his own. So now the poor fellow has only mutilation as reward for his night's work."

When I heard this I froze with horror. I tested my condition. I clutched at my nose; it came off in my hand. I felt my ears; they fell to the ground. Everyone was staring at me, pointing at me, or nodding "I told you so!" and roaring with laughter. In a cold sweat I forced my way through the crowd and made my escape. And afterwards I could not bring myself to return, helpless and a general butt of mockery, to my fathers' home. I let my hair grow long at the sides to hide the stumps of my ears, and I decently covered my shameful nose with this adhesive linen patch.

As soon as Thelyphron had told his story, all the party, now far gone in wine, laughed heartily. . . .

THE STORY OF
THE GENTLEWOMAN
BY APULEIUS

This story from *The Golden Ass,* like the preceding one,
has been translated by Morris Bishop.

[Lucius, the narrator, is turned by black magic into an ass.
He becomes the burden-bearer of a band of robbers, with their
headquarters in a cave.]

THE THIEVES returned to the cave, downcast and distressed. They carried no bundles of booty, not even a
common cloak. They had taken nothing by the craft and
violence of the whole robber band except one poor girl,
who seemed by her dress to be a gentlewoman, even of the
ruling class of the region. She was such a girl, I swear, as
could rouse the emotions even of an ass. The men brought
her in weeping and tearing at her hair and clothes. Once in
the cave, they tried to calm her down, saying: "Your life
and honor are quite safe. Just be patient a while till we can
take our profit. It's poverty and need that have driven us to
this business. Your parents are stingy indeed, but they will
soon loosen their hold on their piles of money and pay a
proper ransom for their dear daughter."

But such cajolements did nothing to banish the girl's
distress. Far from it! She bowed her head down and wept
and wept. The robbers summoned the old woman, their
cook, and ordered her to sit down by the girl and talk her
into sense as far as possible. Then they went off on their
usual business. The girl would not be distracted from her
grieving by any words of the old woman, but, screaming

and racking her breast with sobs, she made even me weep. "Oh, how unhappy I am!" she cried. "To have lost my home, my family, my loving slaves, my pious parents! And now I am the prey of kidnappers, a mere piece of property! And I'm shut in this stone prison like a slave, with none of the comforts I was born and bred to! I don't know what will become of me. Among these bloody butchers, these thieves and horrid assassins, how can I cease to weep, how can I hope to live?"

Thus did she lament; and worn out with grief, with screaming, and with bodily exhaustion, she closed her drooping eyes in sleep. But after only a brief repose she suddenly awoke and sprang up like a frantic woman, and began to afflict herself even more violently, beating her breast cruelly and smiting her lovely face. The old woman pressed her to tell the reason for this new access of grief. She heaved a deep sigh and replied: "Alas, now I am certainly and surely destroyed! Now there is no more hope for me. There is nothing left for me but a rope, or a sword, or a precipice!"

This irritated the old woman, who turned a scowling face to the girl and bade her tell what new misfortune she was bewailing, and why, after a moment's doze, she had started squalling and bawling again. "No doubt you think you can cheat my boys out of their just fee for your ransom," she said. "If you keep this up, I'll have you burned alive. Little the robbers care for those tears."

Terrified by these words, the girl kissed the old woman's hands. "Pardon me, good mother!" she said. "Wait a little, and show some human pity for my sad case. For surely sympathy is not dead in you, with your long experience and your reverend gray hairs. Let me sketch to you my misfortunes. My betrothed is a handsome youth, outstanding among all his companions. He is the darling of the whole city, and my cousin, three years older than I. We were brought up together from babyhood, lodged in the same room, even in the same bed, and were pledged to one another by mutual affection. He was destined legally by formal engagement to be my husband; the contract was already recorded with parental consent. The wedding day came; the relatives and guests crowded the temples and public buildings and offered sacrifices. Our house was hung with laurel and illumined with torches, while the wedding songs were sung. My mother took me on her lap, dressing me decently in nuptial finery, and covered me with honeyed kisses as she confided her heartfelt hopes for children to come.

"And then suddenly a band of savage-looking armed cutthroats burst in, drawn swords in hand! But they were not intent on murder or robbery. In a compact mass they invaded my bedroom. None of our servants fought back, or even made a show of resistance.

"I was snatched, almost unconscious with terror, from my mother's embrace. The wedding was ruined, like that of Hippodamia and Protesilaus. And now my woes are renewed and redoubled by an ugly dream. I seemed to be dragged from my home, my room, my bed. I was violently cast in trackless wastes, where I called on the name of my luckless husband; and he, torn from my arms, robbed of his bride when he was still fresh with ceremonial ointments and crowned with garlands, followed me by the tracks of my ravishers. He raised a shout that his lovely wife was being stolen away and called people to his aid. But one of the robbers, annoyed at his pursuit, picked up a big stone from the ground and threw it at my poor husband and killed him. Terrified by this horrible sight, I woke shuddering from my evil sleep."

The old woman sighed sympathetically at the tearful recital. "Cheer up, my lady," she said. "Don't let yourself be frightened by the vain images of dreams. Visions seen in broad daylight are often to be reckoned false, just as night's visions very often present the contrary of the truth. Thus tears and beatings and even murders in dreams often foretell money and good luck; whereas to dream of laughing, guzzling honey-cakes, or enjoying the delights of Venus often portends despair of mind, weakness of body, and other misfortunes. Let me distract you with a pretty story, an old wives' tale."

[The old woman recounts at length the idyll of Cupid and Psyche.]

Now the robbers returned, loaded with the spoil of some great foray. Some of them, the most enterprising, had been wounded. These were left in our cavern-home to recover. The others were eager to return to another cave where they had deposited the rest of their loot. They snatched a hasty meal, then hauled me out with my friend the horse, with many blows, to carry back the booty. They clubbed us ahead and drove us up hill and down till at nightfall we arrived, exhausted, at the cave. They loaded us with heavy packs, giving us no time to rest, and brought us back in a great hurry, beating me and raising many a weal; they even knocked me down on a stone by the wayside. Then they redoubled their blows to get me up, wounding me in the right leg and left foot. One said: "How long are we going to go on feeding this crippled ass, who has even gone lame now?" And another: "You said it! He brought bad luck with him. We haven't made a good haul since he arrived; we've had nothing but wounds and the loss of our best men." Then said a third: "As soon as he gets home with his load, if he ever does, I'm going to pitch him over the cliff to feed the vultures."

While these sweet fellows were arguing about the manner of my death, we reached home; fear had equipped my hooves with wings. We were quickly unloaded; no attention was paid to our needs, and even the question of my murder was dropped. They ordered out the wounded who had remained behind and went back to fetch the remainder of the spoil, since, they said, the horse and I merely delayed them. Now a very considerable question presented itself to my mind, in contemplation of my threatened decease, and I said to myself: "Why are you standing there, Lucius? Are you waiting for something to turn up? Death, a very ugly death, is in the offing for you, by the robbers' decree. And it won't cause them any great trouble. Can't you see that nearby cliff, and the sharp rocks at the foot with their jagged flints, which will impale you when you reach bottom? For that marvellous magic has given you the look and the duties of an ass, but not an ass's thick hide—just a skin as tender as that of a leech. Why don't you summon up a man's courage, and look to your salvation when you can? Now you have your best chance to escape, while the robbers are absent. Are you afraid of your guardian, an old hag already half dead? You could finish her off with one good kick, even with your lame leg. But what rescuers can you flee to? Ho! A silly question indeed, a properly asinine question! What traveler, seeing an ass running loose, won't gladly mount him?"

So I gave a sudden jerk to my halter rope and pulled it loose; and I took off at full speed. But I couldn't dodge the vigilance of the hawk-eyed old woman. When she saw me freed she grabbed my rope with an energy surprising in one of her sex and age. I was so conscious of the robbers' grim designs upon me that I showed her no pity; I let her have a mighty kick with my two hind feet and brought her low. But although she lay flat she clung resolutely to my rope and was dragged along for some distance; and she began to yell for help from some stronger hands. But she shouted and screamed in vain; there was no one there who could come to her aid, excepting only the captive girl. She ran up at the outcry and saw, by Hercules, a rare dramatic sight —an aged Dirce dragged not by a bull but by an ass. She plucked up her courage and dared a noble deed worthy of a man. She pulled my halter-rope from the old woman's hands, called to me with soothing words, jumped lightly on my back, and urged me again into a run. Impelled by my own eagerness to escape and by my zeal to rescue the girl, and also influenced by the kicks with which she belabored my flanks, I attained a speed to match that of a race-horse, hardly touching the ground; and I tried to bray an answer to her sweet words. And sometimes, under color of nipping my own back, I bent round my head and kissed her pretty feet.

Then she heaved a deep sigh and gazed aloft in supplication. "O gods above, deliver me, I pray, from my present perils; and do thou, cruel Fortune, abate thy rage; surely thou hast been appeased by my sufferings. And you, dear donkey, guardian of my liberty and safety, if you bring me unharmed to my parents and to my beautiful spouse, what thanks will I give you, with what honors will I crown you, what dinners will I bring you! First I will have your mane properly curried and adorned with my girlhood necklaces, and I will have your forelock curled and neatly parted, and

I will wash and comb the hairs of your tail, now so clotted and horrid, and I'll bespangle you with golden balls, sparkling like stars in the sky, and you will march in triumph in the great festivals, and every day I'll bring you almonds and sweeties in my silk apron; I'll feed you well, my preserver. And in addition to plenty of food and no work you will have honor and glory. For I shall make a perpetual commemoration of my present good fortune and the favor of providence. I shall dedicate a picture of our present escape in the atrium of my home. Everyone will come to see it and will hear the story, which may be simple, but it will be recorded by many a learned scholar as 'The Escape of the Royal Virgin on Ass-Back.' You will be numbered among the ancient miracles; your example will attest the truth of Phrixus' rescue from drowning by a ram, of Arion's ride on a dolphin, of Europa's career on a bull. And if it is true that Jupiter bellowed in bull's form, maybe in my donkey is concealed the figure of a man or a god."

Thus the girl maundered on, mingling sighs and sobs with prayers. We came then to a parting of the road. She pulled at my halter and tried hard to guide me to the right, which was the route to her parents' home. But I was aware that the robbers had gone that way to bring back the remainder of their booty, and I resisted vigorously and mentally protested: "Wretched girl, what are you doing? Why are you hurrying to your doom? Why try to force me, while I stand firm and fixed? You are going to destroy yourself, and me too!" Thus we pointed in opposite directions, like lawyers disputing a property case, or an inheritance. Then suddenly there before us were the thieves, loaded with their ill-gotten gains! They caught sight of us at some distance in the bright moonlight and greeted us with evil laughter. "Whither away in such a hurry?" one shouted. "Aren't you afraid of the ghosts and ghouls that fly by night? My virtuous young lady, were you off to pay a call on your parents? You need protection, all alone like that; we'll give you an escort and show you the best road home!" Another seized me by the halter and turned me around, without sparing blows with a knotty stick he was carrying. Thus, heading back toward my looming fate, I remembered my injured foot and began to limp and bob my head. But the man who held my halter said: "Oho! Now you're stumbling and staggering, are you? Your sore feet could run away all right, and now they can't walk! A minute ago you were beating winged Pegasus for speed!" The jolly joker thus exercised his wit, while pounding me with his stick.

Thus we arrived at the defenses of the robbers' roost. And there from a branch of a tall cypress tree the old woman hung in a noose! They cut her down on the spot, tied her up with the suicidal rope, and tossed her over the cliff. Then they bound the girl fast, and attacked with savage gusto the dinner which the poor old woman had so faithfully prepared for posthumous consumption.

When they had greedily devoured all, they set to a discussion of the proper punishment for our misbehavior. There were various opinions, naturally enough, in such a headstrong company. One was in favor of burning the girl alive; a second proposed throwing her to the wild beasts; a third advocated hanging her on a gibbet; a fourth recommended flaying her alive, with special tortures. At least they all agreed unanimously on her death. Then one succeeded in dominating the discussion, and thus began in a cool ponderous manner: "It would not be fitting to the rules of our Order, nor to the humanity of us as individuals, nor to my own unworthiness, to impose a penalty dispro-

portionate to the crime, and to have recourse to fire, cruci-
fixion, torture, exposure to wild beasts, or to any indecent
abridgment of her punishment. Listen then to my counsel:
grant the girl her life, but only according to her just deserts. You have not forgotten the decree of death you have
already imposed upon this ass, always a shirker, but of
gluttonous appetite. He is also an equivocator; though he
pretends to be lame he has been the agent and accomplice
of the girl's escape. I recommend therefore that tomorrow
his throat be cut, that his vitals be removed, and that to
replace them the girl—whom he has preferred to our company—be stripped naked and sewn into his skin in such
manner that only her head shall emerge, but the rest of her
body be contained within the beast. Then let us expose the
ass, with his human stuffing, on some jagged rock, and
present him to the burning beams of the sun. Thus both of
them will suffer all the penal retribution which you have so
justly proposed. The ass will undergo his well-merited execution; the girl will be mangled by wild beasts and devoured by worms; she will be tortured by fire, when the
sun's heat roasts her in the beast's belly; she will know the
gibbet's punishments, when dogs and vultures tear at her
entrails. Reflect, I beg, on her other torments and tribula-
tions. She will inhabit, living, the body of a dead beast. The
heat will torture her with an intolerable stink. She will
waste away with unappeasable hunger. Nor can she find
any quicker death by her own agency, for her hands will
be bound fast."

The robbers acclaimed these words with whole-hearted
applause and general stamping. I took it all in with my
great ears, and I bewailed inwardly the corpse I would
become next day.

[A robber who had been separated from the band returns,
with news of the city.]

The newcomer pulled out a thousand gold pieces, which he had sewn into his coat-lining. These, he said, he had extricated from the possession of several travelers, and in all honesty, as he put it, he was contributing them to the common treasury. He then inquired solicitously about the welfare of the company. He was informed that a number of the companions had met their death, though very gallantly, in various valiant enterprises. He recommended that all forays should be suspended for a time and the highways be left in peace, and that rather all efforts should be bent to the recruitment of new comrades in arms, that by the enlistment of likely youths the martial band might be brought up to full strength. He judged that the unwilling might be terrified into joining and that the willing might be encouraged by the promise of profit. A good many, he said, would renounce the humble life of a slave, preferring to join a comity where all were as mighty as kings. He had himself happened to encounter a tall young man, big-bodied and ready with his fists. He had argued with the youth and had at length persuaded him to use his strength, which had long lain idle, for a better purpose, to enjoy, while still he might, the benefits of his vigor, and instead of holding out his hand for a beggarly pittance, to appropriate gold to his desire.

All agreed with these proposals. They voted that the man who had already been interviewed be recruited and that others be sounded out, to fill out the cadre. The returned member went out and reappeared shortly after, as he had promised, with a tall, even enormous young man. He dwarfed the whole band, overtopping them by a head and surpassing all in breadth of shoulder, though only a downy beard covered his cheeks. But he was dressed in rags and patches clumsily sewn together, gaping to reveal his broad breast and hard belly.

"Hail!" said the youth on entering. "Hail, associates of the mighty god Mars, and now my faithful comrades in arms! Receive willingly, I pray you, a willing and vigorous recruit. I will risk wounds on my body for money in my hand; and I'll take my chances of death, which others fear so much. Don't think me a dead-beat beggar, don't judge my quality by these rags. I was captain of a powerful company, with which I laid waste all Macedonia. I am that famous bandit Haemus the Thracian, whose name is the terror of a whole province. My father was Theron, also a very eminent brigand. I was suckled on human blood and educated by the robber bands to be the heir and emulator of my father's merits. But I lost the command of my powerful cohort and all its rich stores in a few brief hours. For without the gods' favor I mounted an attack on a captain, an imperial functionary, who had tucked away some two hundred gold pieces and had then got into trouble. But let me tell the story from the beginning.

"In Caesar's court there was a certain distinguished and honored man, holding many posts, and respected by the Emperor himself. But envious rivals cunningly fabricated accusations and brought about his banishment. His wife was Plotina, a woman of rare fidelity and singular virtue, who had contributed ten children to her husband's household. She scorned and rejected all the charms of Roman luxury, shared her spouse's exile and disgrace, cut her hair and put on men's clothes, strapped on a money-belt filled with gold and her most precious jewels, and thus fearlessly passed through the cordon of guards with their drawn swords. She shared all her husband's dangers, watched vigilantly over his safety, and endured many hardships with a truly manly spirit. Now after many long and difficult wanderings and terrors and sufferings by sea he neared the island of Zacynthus, which an evil fate had designated as his temporary sojourn. The party arrived at the seacoast of Actium, where we were operating after leaving Macedonia. They disembarked late at night and took refuge in a *taverna* near the ship, and there they slept, to escape the sea's tossing. Well, we broke in and made a clean sweep of things; and really we were in no small danger before we made off. For the matron heard the first squeak of the door; she ran into the bedroom and gave a general alarm with her screams. She roused up the armed guards and the servants, calling each by name, and brought the neighbors in on the run. Being outnumbered, every man of us looked to his own welfare and faded away, but it was only by good luck that we all escaped. Then this saintly woman—I must give her her due—being totally devoted to her husband and universally esteemed for her character, made appeal to the divine power of Caesar; and she obtained the prompt return to court of her husband and the assurance of full punishment of our aggression. In short, Caesar willed that Haemus' fraternity should cease to exist; and it very quickly collapsed. Such is the power of Great Caesar's nod! My company was hunted down by detachments of the military, cut up and destroyed.

"I alone stole away and barely escaped the yawning jaws of hell, and in this manner. I put on a woman's flowered dress falling in loose folds, with a close-woven coif on my head, and on my feet those white slippers women wear; and thus lightly costumed and hidden under the aspect of the weaker sex I mounted an ass loaded with barley-sheaves. I passed through a line of hostile soldiers; they let me through freely, thinking me just a donkey-girl, for my cheeks were still hairless and in a boyish bloom. But I did not disavow my father's glory or my own manliness, though I admit I was nervous among all those drawn swords. Protected by my disguise, I invaded country-houses and fortified manors all alone, and scraped together a little travel-money."

At this he cut open part of his ragged dress and poured forth two thousand gold pieces. "Here," he said, "is my contribution, or better my entrance fee, to your corporation. And I offer myself freely as candidate for your honorable captaincy, if you will accept me. And I propose before long to wall this stony home with gold."

On the spot, with a unanimous vote, the robbers elected him captain. They draped him in a magnificent robe to replace the rags which had concealed his wealth. Thus transmogrified, he saluted each and all with a kiss, then took the high seat at the head of the table and commenced a round of healths. Then the talk turned on the young woman's escape and my service as her transport. The new captain learned of the horrid death projected for us both. He inquired where she was held. Being led to the spot and seeing her fast bound, he turned aside with a sniff, and said: "I am not so unreasonable or so rash as to oppose your decisions; but I would feel a twinge of guilty conscience if I should conceal from you my own conviction as to the best course to follow. Please believe that I am animated solely by concern for your welfare. If my proposal does not meet with your approval, you can always return to the ass-immolation project. I judge that thieves, if they are sensible, should prize profit above all, especially above revenge, which is so likely to misfire and injure the wrong persons. Consider therefore that if you destroy this girl by ass-implantation, you will reap no profit except the satisfaction of your own resentment. I propose therefore to take her to some city and there sell her. For this girl, so young and tender, would bring a high price. I have some very good friends in the pimping line; one of them, I am sure, will pay very dear for this girl and put her in a high-class brothel; you can be sure she won't run away from him. When she is working in his bawdy-house you will have vengeance aplenty on her. I have stated my honest and sincere opinion as to the profitable course; but naturally you are free to decide about your own property."

Thus that excellent robber, pleading the interests of the treasury, pled our own case and loomed as savior to the maiden and her ass. The others deliberated for a long time, keeping my heart and soul in torture. Finally they rallied to the opinion of the new-recruited thief, and loosed the maiden from her shackles. But when she looked at the youth and heard his talk of brothels and pimps, she began to laugh very gayly; so that I justly regarded all women alike with loathing, to see a girl, after pretending love for a young suitor and desire for a chaste marriage, suddenly show pleasure at the idea of a foul and filthy brothel! Indeed, the entire female sex and its morals stood condemned in my—of course asinine—view.

The young man made a further suggestion. "Why not make supplication to Comrade Mars and at the same time see about selling the girl and recruiting new members? Apparently we have here no proper beasts for sacrifice or even sufficient drinkable wine. So detail ten companions for me, enough for me to take to the next town, and I'll bring back a proper feast for priests of Mars." Thus his expedition started off, and the others built a great fire and an altar of green turfs in honor of Mars.

Not long after they returned, carrying wine-skins and driving a herd of beasts with many curses. They picked out a big ram, old and hairy, and sacrificed him to Mars, their aide and comrade. They then prepared a noble banquet. The newcomer declared: "You ought to consider me not only captain of our expeditions and robberies, but also leader of your diversions." Taking the initiative, he organized everything most efficiently. He swept out the cave, he laid the table, he cooked the dinner, he chopped up the meat and served it elegantly; but chiefly he kept everyone's big wine-cup filled to the brim. And sometimes, pretending to fetch some article in demand, he took pains to visit the girl, and brought her some dainty abstracted from the table, and gayly offered her drink from cups his lips had already touched. And she accepted them readily; and sometimes, when he made a move to kiss her, she returned his kisses with apparent alacrity. All this offended me extremely; I muttered: "So, virgin maid, you have forgotten your bridal and your mutual vows? And you prefer this blood-stained interloper to the husband destined for you by your parents? Doesn't your conscience prick you, when you toss away your great love to play the harlot among all these swords and spears? What if the thieves should learn of your behavior? Wouldn't you look again to the ass to save you and again bring about my destruction? You're playing your own game, but you're wagering another creature's skin!"

While I was indulging in these angry but rather rhetorical apostrophes, I began to recognize from certain exchanges between the two, comprehensible to a really intelligent ass, that the young man was not Haemus the famous brigand but Tlepolemus, the girl's bridegroom. For he began to speak more openly, paying no more heed to me than if I were dead. "Cheer up, my sweet Charite!" he said. "Soon you'll have all your enemies under lock and key!" He kept pouring out the strong wine, undiluted and slightly warmed, till the brigands were staggering drunk, while he took hardly a drop. And, egad, he made me suspect that he had mixed in some potent sleeping-draught. Finally all of them without exception collapsed, overcome with wine, and lay as if dead. And with no trouble at all he bound them tightly, and when he judged them helpless he set the girl on my back and set off to his home.

When we arrived there all the citizens turned out to see the answer to their prayers. The parents ran up, and the relatives, friends, fosterlings, slaves, all beaming with joy. It was a veritable celebration, of both sexes and all ages, gathered to inspect, by Hercules, a novel and ever-memorable sight—a virgin riding in triumph on an ass. And I too rejoiced in my most manly manner, and to make no discord in the celebration pricked up my long ears, blew out my nostrils, and brayed a terrific blast; or to be exact, I out-thundered a thunderclap. The girl's parents established her in her room and tended her needs solicitously. And Tlepolemus assembled hastily a great posse of citizens and beasts of burden, including me, to my great pleasure, for I was very eager to see the capture of the thieves. We found them still bound fast, but more by wine than by ropes. All their possessions were recovered and brought forth. We were all loaded down with gold and silver and other prizes; and some of the robbers, still fettered, were thrown over the nearby precipice onto the rocks of the chasm, while others were put to the sword and left to rot.

Happy and gay at this vengeance, we returned to the city. The recovered property was deposited in the public treasury, and the rescued girl was legally united to Tlepolemus. She made much of me, calling me her savior; and on the formal wedding day she had my manger filled with barley, and provided a ration of hay sufficient for a Bactrian camel. . . .

ANDROCLUS AND THE LION

BY AULUS GELLIUS

Aulus Gellius was born sometime about A.D. 123, and died soon after 169. He was apparently of an aristocratic, well-to-do family. He had a thorough literary education in Rome, finishing off with a year or more in Athens. There he began his *Noctes Atticæ*, an assemblage of miscellaneous notes, largely on points of grammar, literature, and law.

His story of Androclus and the lion has had a new birth and life in the deft hands of George Bernard Shaw. Our translation is by Morris Bishop.

A PION, called Plistonices, was a sound literary scholar with an especially wide knowledge of Greek culture. His books have a certain standing; they contain a summary of all the remarkable sights and scenes of Egypt. When he reports what he has heard or read he is perhaps unduly verbose, being all too eager to display his learning—he has the scholar's auto-intoxication with his own words. But this story, recorded in his *Egypt and the Egyptians*, is not second-hand, but is something he saw with his own eyes in Rome.

Says he: "One day a great Battle of the Beasts was staged in the Circus Maximus for the popular pleasure. As I happened to be in Rome, I attended. Many savage animals were shown there, some of them enormous and all unusual either in their character or in their ferocity. Among them all one of the lions stood out, to general wonder, by his huge size. This lion drew all eyes to him because of his great agile body, his terrific thunderous roar, his swelling muscles, and his tossing mane.

"Then the men designated to fight the wild beasts were led in. Among them was the slave of a consul; his name was Androclus. And the lion, on perceiving him, stopped as if in surprise. And then he walked up to the man slowly and quietly, as if half-recognizing him. Then he wagged his tail in a placating manner, like a dog fawning on a friend, and came up to the man—now nearly senseless with fright— and gently licked his feet and hands. The man Androclus bore the caresses of the horrid beast, gradually recovered his lost wits, and ventured to regard him closely. Then one could witness a scene of mutual recognition, with man and lion joyfully greeting one another."

At this extraordinary sight, says Apion, the spectators burst out in a terrific shout; and Gaius Caesar himself summoned Androclus and asked him why that most savage lion had spared him alone. Then Androclus told a remarkable and amazing story. Said he: "When my master was appointed proconsul of his province, I suffered unjust daily beatings at his hands. I was driven to run away, and in order to find safer refuge from my master the governor I sought out the solitudes of the fields and deserts. I fully intended to welcome death in some manner, if I should run short of food. Then when the midday sun was blazing fiercely I discovered a secluded, shady cave. There I entered and hid. And shortly afterward this lion came in, limping on a bloody foot, moaning and whimpering, and manifesting the torturing pain of his wound."

The man said that at his first glimpse of the approaching lion he was frightened almost to death. "But," he said, "after the lion came in to what was apparently his den and saw me cowering as far away as I could get, he came up all kindly and gentle and lifted up his paw to show it to me, and seemed to be begging my help. Then I pulled out a huge thorn stuck in his paw, and I squeezed out the pus that had accumulated inside the wound, and losing my fear I wiped away the blood and cleaned out the injured place. Relieved by my treatment and cure, he put his paw in my hand, lay down, and went to sleep.

"From that day on for a good three years the lion and I lived together in that cave, sharing our food. When he made a kill he would bring the best bits home to our cave; and as I had no way of making a fire, I would toast the meat in the midday sun before eating it. But eventually I got bored with that savage existence; and one day when my lion was off on a hunt I left the cave. After a three days' walk I was seen and picked up by some soldiers. I was shipped from Africa to my master in Rome. He immediately had me condemned to death by being thrown to the beasts. And now I recognize that this lion, who must have been captured after we parted, is thanking me for my kindness and my physicking."

Thus Apion reports Androclus' story. It was all written down on a tablet, which was carried about the Circus and read aloud to the spectators. All petitioned that Androclus should be released and acquitted, and voted that the lion should be presented to him. "Afterwards," says Apion, "we used to see Androclus with his lion on a flimsy leash, making the rounds of the bars. Androclus took up collections, his lion was crowned with flowers, and everyone he met would declare: 'There goes the lion who took in the man, and there goes the lion's doctor!' "

A CLASSICAL STORYBOOK

Designed by R. E. Rosenbaum.
Composed by Kingsport Press, Inc.,
in 11 point linotype Janson, 3 points leaded,
with display lines in Augustea Inline and Palatino.
Printed from letterpress plates by Kingsport Press, Inc.,
on Warren's Olde Style India, 60 pound basis,
with the Cornell University Press watermark.
Bound by Kingsport Press, Inc.,
in Interlaken Arco 3 Linen-smooth
and stamped in imitation gold foil.